Editor
Nancy Hoffman

Managing Editor
Karen J. Goldfluss, M.S. Ed.

Cover Artist
Brenda DiAntonis

Illustrator
Kevin McCarthy

Art Production Manager
Kevin Barnes

Art Coordinator
Renée Christine Yates

Imaging
James Edward Grace
Rosa C. See

Publisher
Mary D. Smith, M.S. Ed.

Spotlight On
AMERICA

Grades 5 & Up

20th Century Wars

Author

Robert W. Smith

Teacher Created Resources, Inc.
6421 Industry Way
Westminster, CA 92683
www.teachercreated.com

ISBN: 978-1-4206-3219-4

©2006 Teacher Created Resources, Inc.
Reprinted, 2012
Made in U.S.A.

Table of Contents

Introduction

The *Spotlight on America* series is designed to introduce significant events in American history to students. Reading in the content area is enriched with a variety of activities in language arts, literature, social studies, oral and written expression, math, science, and physical education. The series is designed to make history literally come alive in your classroom and take root in the minds of your students.

The 20th century was a watershed in human history for both good and evil. Medical advances and technological inventions resulted in a longer life span, an abundance of food and clothing, and limitless opportunities for leisure and recreation. It was a century of great learning and advancement for many people and societies.

In the same century, however, war became more terrible than ever. Medical treatment cannot keep up with the machinery of killing. The carnage of the 20th century was enormous in terms of lives lost and devastated in wars or military conflicts. The technology of war became so lethal that entire nations lost one or more generations of their young men on the fields of death.

In addition, the social and revolutionary dislocation created by these hostilities ripped apart the fabric of societies throughout the world. Some cultures and people groups were destroyed by accident, and many others were ravaged by genocide. Racial and religious hatreds flared into hostilities involving people around the world. War was an instrument of repression for some people and liberation for others. The United States' economy, culture, and democratic institutions were profoundly impacted and challenged by these conflicts.

The reading selections in this book introduce the major conflicts of the 20th century—especially those which directly impacted Americans—and also set the stage for learning activities in other subject areas. The literature activities are intended to bring students into the lives of people who endured war, relocation, the Holocaust, and the suffering of refugees. The language arts, social studies, science, and math activities are designed to help students become aware of and empathize with the people who lived through these hostilities. The culminating activities aim to acquaint students with the life and times during these wars and conflict.

Enjoy using this book with your students. Look for other books in this series.

Teacher Lesson Plans for Reading Comprehension

World War I: Early Stages

Objective: Students will demonstrate fluency and comprehension in reading historically based text.

Materials: copies of World War I: Early Stages (pages 8–10); copies of World War I: Early Stages Quiz (page 28); additional reading selections from books, encyclopedias, and Internet sources for enrichment

Procedure

1. Reproduce and distribute World War I: Early Stages. Review pre-reading skills by briefly reviewing the text and encouraging students to underline, make notes in the margins, write questions, and highlight unfamiliar words as they read.

2. Have students read the article independently, in small groups, or together as a class.

3. As a class, discuss the following questions or others of your choosing.

   • What do you think was the most important cause of World War I?

   • Could these same causes start a world war now?

   • What was life like in the trenches of World War I?

Assessment: Have students complete World War I: Early Stages Quiz. Correct the quiz together.

World War I: Later Stages

Objective: Students will demonstrate fluency and comprehension in reading historically based text.

Materials: copies of World War I: Later Stages (pages 11 and 12); copies of World War I: Later Stages Quiz (page 29); additional reading selections from books, encyclopedias, and Internet sources for enrichment

Procedure

1. Reproduce and distribute World War I: Later Stages. Review pre-reading skills by briefly reviewing the text and encouraging students to underline, make notes in the margins, write questions, and highlight unfamiliar words as they read.

2. Have students read the article independently, in small groups, or together as a class.

3. As a class, discuss the following questions or others of your choosing.

   • How would you describe military thinking during World War I?

   • Was the outcome of World War I worth the cost?

   • Should Germany have been punished for starting the war?

Assessment: Have students complete World War I: Later Stages Quiz. Correct the quiz together.

Teacher Lesson Plans for Reading Comprehension *(cont.)*

World War II: Causes

Objective: Students will demonstrate fluency and comprehension in reading historically based text.

Materials: copies of World War II: Causes (pages 13–15); copies of World War II: Causes Quiz (page 30); additional reading selections from books, encyclopedias, and Internet sources for enrichment

Procedure

1. Reproduce and distribute World War II: Causes. Review pre-reading skills by briefly reviewing the text and encouraging students to underline, make notes in the margins, write questions, and highlight unfamiliar words as they read.

2. Have students read the article independently, in small groups, or together as a class.

3. As a class, discuss the following questions or others of your choosing.

   • What was the most important cause of World War II?

   • How did the rise of dictatorships lead to war?

   • Why were most countries, except for Germany, unprepared for war?

Assessment: Have students complete World War II: Causes Quiz. Correct the quiz together.

World War II: The Fighting

Objective: Students will demonstrate fluency and comprehension in reading historically based text.

Materials: copies of World War II: The Fighting (pages 16 and 17); copies of World War II: The Fighting Quiz (page 31); additional reading selections from books, encyclopedias, and Internet sources for enrichment

Procedure

1. Reproduce and distribute World War II: The Fighting. Review pre-reading skills by briefly reviewing the text and encouraging students to underline, make notes in the margins, write questions, and highlight unfamiliar words as they read.

2. Have students read the article independently, in small groups, or together as a class.

3. As a class, discuss the following questions or others of your choosing.

   • Why was the U.S. called the "arsenal of democracy?"

   • What was Germany's greatest military blunder during the war? Give your reasons.

   • Was World War II worth the cost in lives and resources? Why?

Assessment: Have students complete World War II: The Fighting Quiz. Correct the quiz together.

Teacher Lesson Plans for Reading Comprehension *(cont.)*

The Korean War

Objective: Students will demonstrate fluency and comprehension in reading historically based text.

Materials: copies of The Korean War (pages 18 and 19); copies of The Korean War Quiz (page 32); additional reading selections from books, encyclopedias, and Internet sources for enrichment

Procedure

1. Reproduce and distribute The Korean War. Review pre-reading skills by briefly reviewing the text and encouraging students to underline, make notes in the margins, write questions, and highlight unfamiliar words as they read.

2. Have students read the article independently, in small groups, or together as a class.

3. As a class, discuss the following questions or others of your choosing.

   • What miscalculations or misunderstandings did the United States make before and during the Korean War?

   • Why would some soldiers not want to return to their own country after the war?

   • Should the United States have continued fighting the Korean War until it won?

Assessment: Have students complete The Korean War Quiz. Correct the quiz together.

The Vietnam War

Objective: Students will demonstrate fluency and comprehension in reading historically based text.

Materials: copies of The Vietnam War (pages 20–23); copies of The Vietnam War Quiz (page 33); additional reading selections from books, encyclopedias, and Internet sources for enrichment

Procedure

1. Reproduce and distribute The Vietnam War. Review pre-reading skills by briefly reviewing the text and encouraging students to underline, make notes in the margins, write questions, and highlight unfamiliar words as they read.

2. Have students read the article independently, in small groups, or together as a class.

3. As a class, discuss the following questions or others of your choosing.

   • What mistakes did the United States make before and during the Vietnam War?

   • Why did North Vietnam win the war?

   • What were the long-term results of the Vietnam War?

Assessment: Have students complete The Vietnam War Quiz. Correct the quiz together.

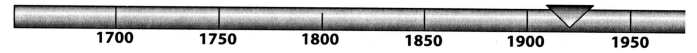

Teacher Lesson Plans for Reading Comprehension *(cont.)*

The Cold War

Objective: Students will demonstrate fluency and comprehension in reading historically based text.

Materials: copies of The Cold War (pages 24 and 25); copies of The Cold War Quiz (page 34); additional reading selections from books, encyclopedias, and Internet resources for enrichment

Procedure

1. Reproduce and distribute The Cold War. Review pre-reading skills by briefly reviewing the text and encouraging students to underline, make notes in the margins, write questions, and highlight unfamiliar words as they read.

2. Have students read the article independently, in small groups, or together as a class.

3. As a class, discuss the following questions or others of your choosing.

   • Why was the Cold War essential to the protection of democracies in the world?

   • What was the greatest danger to the world during the Cold War? Explain your choice.

   • What would have happened if the United States and its allies had not opposed the Soviet Union after World War II?

   • How did victory in World War II lead to the Cold War?

Assessment: Have students complete The Cold War Quiz. Correct the quiz together.

Other 20th Century Conflicts

Objective: Students will demonstrate fluency and comprehension in reading historically based text.

Materials: copies of Other 20th Century Conflicts (pages 26 and 27); copies of the Other 20th Century Conflicts Quiz (page 35); additional reading selections from books, encyclopedias, and Internet resources for enrichment

Procedure

1. Reproduce and distribute Other 20th Century Conflicts. Review pre-reading skills by briefly reviewing the text and encouraging students to underline, make notes in the margins, write questions, and highlight unfamiliar words as they read.

2. Have students read the article independently, in small groups, or together as a class.

3. As a class, discuss the following questions or others of your choosing.

   • Why is the Arab-Israeli conflict so difficult to solve?

   • How did Saddam Hussein affect war and peace in the Middle East?

   • How did the Balkan conflicts lead to World War I?

   • Why do you think the Balkan conflicts are difficult to solve so that all of the nations involved are satisfied?

Assessment: Have students complete the Other 20th Century Conflicts Quiz. Correct the quiz together.

 Reading Passages

World War I: Early Stages

Causes of World War I

The nations of Europe blundered into World War I. They did not intend to start a war, but their actions created the conditions that caused one. Although there had been some brief and limited wars in the 19th century, the great powers of Europe—England, France, Germany, Austria-Hungary, and Russia—had enjoyed a century of relative peace before 1914. They had accomplished this through a series of alliances designed to keep a delicate balance of power in Europe.

European Rivalries

However, these European nations had become large empires competing fiercely for shares of the world's trade. They battled for colonies in Africa and Asia because these colonies were a source of wealth, cheap labor, and essential materials for industry and war. They also provided a sense of power and pride.

The rivalries between countries were also increased by the personal conflicts among the monarchs of Europe. Nearly all of these kings and queens were cousins or closely related by blood or marriage. Most were related to Queen Victoria of England, who married her many children to rulers throughout Europe. She hoped this would encourage peace. Instead, the family bickering increased the potential for war.

The growth of extreme *nationalism*, devotion to a country, also created bitter racial and ethnic resentments between nations and within empires like Austria-Hungary, where many ethnic and religious groups lived together uneasily. This extreme nationalism made it easier to raise armies at the beginning of the war since each nation thought it was naturally superior to all the others.

Alliances

These intense rivalries caused several nations to form alliances to protect them from potential enemies. The *Triple Alliance* was made up of Germany, Italy, and Austria-Hungary. These countries agreed to defend each other if one of them was attacked.

In response, the *Triple Entente* was formed by Britain, France, and Russia to counter any attack upon each other. These nations had also created powerful armies and navies. They claimed their military build-up was for self-defense, but each nation suspected other nations were preparing for aggression. The stage was set for world war. If one nation went to war, all of its allies would quickly become involved in the war because of these entangling alliances.

These alliances would change somewhat during World War I, however. The Triple Alliance dissolved, and a new coalition was formed. It was called the *Central Powers* and consisted of Germany, Austria-Hungary, the Ottoman Empire (present day Turkey), and Bulgaria. The Triple Entente expanded and became known as the *Allies*. The Allies included Great Britain, Russia, Serbia, Japan, Belgium, Italy, the United States, France, Greece, Romania, Australia, Canada, and New Zealand.

World War I: Early Stages *(cont.)*

The Spark of War

"The war to end all wars," as World War I was later referred to, began with a public murder. The assassination of Archduke Franz Ferdinand of Austria by a Serbian fanatic led to a declaration of war on July 28, 1914, by Austria-Hungry who thought Serbia had encouraged this act of terrorism against it.

Once started, the fire of war spread out of control. Russia was allied to Serbia so it declared war on Austria-Hungary. Germany was allied to Austria-Hungary and fearful of Russia so Germany declared war on Russia on August 1, 1914.

France mobilized its army, which led Germany to declare war on France on August 3, 1914, partly because the *mobilization*, or preparation and movement, of an army was basically seen as an act of war itself. When Germany invaded Belgium on its way to war with the French army, Great Britain declared war on Germany on August 4, 1914. Since Japan had an alliance with Britain, it joined the Allies (formerly the Triple Entente) three weeks later.

The Ottoman Empire joined Germany and the Central Powers. Italy left the Triple Alliance and remained neutral until later in the war when it joined Britain and her allies. The United States, which had avoided entangling alliances, remained neutral until attacks on American ships compelled it to join Britain and the Allies against the Central Powers in 1917.

Germany Invades Belgium

The Germans had planned well. They launched a surprise offensive through Belgium and attacked France along its undefended border with Belgium. Germany intended to use its invading army to pin down France's forces, and it almost worked. They were stopped, however, by fierce resistance from French and British forces at the First Battle of Marne along the Marne River. Both sides dug in, and a series of intense battles began. This war in the trenches resulted in millions of casualties but little movement of the opposing armies over the next four years.

 Reading Passages

World War I: Early Stages *(cont.)*

Trench Warfare

Military tactics at the beginning of World War I were centered around two main elements: enormous firepower and rapid movement of troops. Machine guns, powerful cannons that could fire huge explosives at great distances, and concentrated rifle fire were designed to provide cover for soldiers who attacked enemy lines in quick surges and then battled in hand-to-hand bayonet fights. (*Bayonets* are knives attached to the barrel of a rifle so that the rifle can be used like a spear at close range.)

The war quickly settled into a fight for narrow pieces of the battlefield with men charging into massive firepower from machine guns, rifles, and cannons. Both attackers and defenders used hand grenades and rifles, but the attackers were always at greater risk. They suffered terrible casualties to gain extremely minor parcels of land.

The trenches were filled with muddy water, human waste, rats, insects, wounded soldiers, and the mangled bodies of the dead. Lice fed on the living soldiers, and rats fed on the dead and dying. Some of the trenches were used as long as four years and were occupied by different armies at different stages in the war.

Life in the Trenches

The death rate in the trenches was extremely high. The soldiers who fought in these trenches suffered horribly. If they were wounded during a daytime attack, they were often left on the battlefield until survivors could be picked up under the cover of darkness. Disease and infections were spread to almost every soldier. Huge numbers of soldiers died from disease rather than battlefield injuries. Medical care was still primitive, and soldiers often lost arms or legs which might have been saved with proper treatment.

Another horrible practice was the use of poisonous chemicals such as mustard gas and chlorine gas that were fired at enemy trenches with artillery shells. Soldiers had to wear gas masks to avoid painful injuries, disfigurement, and death. Mustard gas was the most lethal of the poisonous chemicals used during World War I. It blisters the skin of victims, irritates the eyes, causes vomiting and internal and external bleeding, and attacks the bronchial tubes. Chlorine gas destroys the respiratory organs of its victims, which leads to a slow death by asphyxiation. An estimated 91,000 soldiers died as a result of poison gas attacks, and another 1.2 million were hospitalized.

 Reading Passages

World War I: Later Stages

Battles at Tannenberg and Masurian Lakes

While Germany was attacking France, two separate Russian armies attacked Austria-Hungary and East Prussia. The Russian armies were huge, but they were very poorly trained, equipped, and led. The two Russian commanders hated each other and did not cooperate well. Messages were sent over wireless radio transmitters and were not coded, which enabled them to be intercepted. The German army essentially destroyed both Russian armies, first at Tannenberg and later at Masurian Lakes.

Verdun

By 1916 the German commander-in-chief had decided to attack and destroy the famous complex of fortresses at Verdun, which controlled access to eastern France. The intent was to kill huge numbers of French troops and end the stalemate which had developed. In February 1916, the Germans launched massive attacks against the French at Verdun and sent waves of troops to wipe out the French defenders. French reinforcements were sent in, and Germany made few real gains. With their rallying cry of "They shall not pass!" the French were able to keep the Germans from advancing. Losses on both sides were high. The battle cost the French 400,000 casualties and the Germans about 320,000 casualties.

Bloodbath at the Somme

The British hoped to break the stalemate near the Somme River in northeastern France. They launched a massive artillery barrage of 1.6 million artillery shells against the entrenched German forces. The German troops moved underground and avoided most of the damage from the barrage. The British troop advance was met with massive force. More than 60,000 British troops were wounded or killed on the first day. When the battle finally ended later in the year, the British had suffered 420,000 casualties, the French lost 195,000, and the German defenders suffered 650,000 casualties. No real progress was made.

Reading Passages

World War I: Later Stages *(cont.)*

Other Battles

A fierce battle was fought in 1915 on the Gallipoli Peninsula in Turkey where British forces were trying to keep open a narrow waterway which supplied Russia. The British forces were defeated by the Turks with a loss of 214,000 British and Allied casualties and 300,000 Turkish soldiers. The British won a bitter and costly sea battle at Jutland near Denmark in June 1916, which gave them clear command of the seas for the rest of the war. The Third Battle at Ypres in Belgium had the same effect as the battles at Verdun and the Somme—massive casualties on both sides but no clear victor.

The End of the War

The Russian army simply dissolved as the war dragged on. By the end of 1917, the Russian army and nation were no longer willing or able to fight. A revolution had removed the tsar, Russia's ruler, from the throne. By early 1918, Russia had signed a peace treaty with Germany.

The U.S. Enters the War

The entrance of the United States into the war turned the tide for the Allies. Two million U.S. troops were sent to France, where they fought as an independent force under American leadership. In a series of battles at the Second Battle of the Marne, Argonne Forest, and St. Michel, the Germans realized that they could not match the American forces. Germany was losing on other fronts as well as in Bulgaria, Turkey, and Italy.

Armistice

The Germans agreed to an *armistice*, or peace agreement, on Allied terms which took effect on November 11, 1918, at 11:00 A.M. World War I, the costliest war in human history up to that time, was finally over. Nearly 10 million soldiers were killed, and at least 21 million more were wounded. No one knows how many civilians were killed or injured by the war, but estimates suggest there were at least as many civilian deaths as military deaths from disease, starvation, and war-related causes. Most of the nations in Europe were financially ruined and owed massive war debts. The Treaty of Versailles, the peace settlement which followed the war, was very punitive toward Germany, and aimed to punish the country. This planted the seeds for a future war.

 Reading Passages

World War II: Causes

The Cost of War

World War II was the most catastrophic war in the history of the world. It killed more people, destroyed more property, and uprooted the lives of more people than any previous war in history. At least 17 million soldiers and more than 35 million civilians were killed. Millions of soldiers were wounded or missing in action. At least 70 million soldiers from more than 70 countries were involved in the conflict.

Casualties resulted from battle, starvation, epidemic diseases, massacres, bombing raids, and the total chaos in war-torn countries with no police and public services. The war was truly a world war in that the battles were fought on the plains of Europe, in the air over oceans and continents, on and under the sea in both major oceans, in the tropical jungles of Africa and Asia, and across much of Europe and Asia.

Causes of World War II

The two principal opponents in World War II were the *Axis* powers comprised of Germany, Japan, and Italy and the *Allies* which included Great Britain, France, the United States, and the Soviet Union (formerly Russia). The root causes of World War II were the rise of dictatorships in Europe and Asia, extreme nationalism, economic depression, aggressive conquest of weaker countries by stronger countries, and the bitter resentment created by the peace treaties which ended World War I.

Rise of Dictatorships and Aggression

The Axis powers were all under the control of dictators who wanted to expand the territories under their control. Germany, led by Adolf Hitler, took over Austria and Czechoslovakia and had intentions of conquering or controlling much larger sections of Europe, Asia, and Africa.

Adolf Hitler

Italy, under Benito Mussolini, conquered Albania and parts of East Africa. Japan, controlled by a small group of military officers, invaded Manchuria, a province of China, in 1931, and by 1938 occupied eastern China. Japan already controlled Korea and intended to dominate the entire Pacific area. In 1941 General Hideki Tojo assumed power in Japan.

Benito Mussolini

Reading Passages

World War II: Causes *(cont.)*

The Peace of Paris

The Treaty of Versailles ending World War I was a major cause of World War II. Germany felt that the war *reparations* (money and land) that it was forced to pay were too severe. Germany also did not want to admit responsibility for starting World War I. As victors, Italy and Japan felt they did not receive enough land. In addition, Japan was insulted by the Europeans' unwillingness to accept the equality of all races.

The Great Depression

The Great Depression began in the United States in 1929 and rapidly spread throughout the world, throwing the economies of all nations into chaos. Many people were out of work or could get only occasional jobs. Most countries did not have provisions to care for the unemployed, and millions of people became victims of poverty. Looking for leaders who would solve their financial woes and offer them a better life, people often became followers of radical political and economic movements.

Fascism and Communism

In the Western world two major political forces fed on people's misery. *Fascism* was a political movement that was strongly nationalistic and favored a powerful central government ruled by a dictator. People in Germany and Italy accepted fascism as a solution to their problems.

Communism was a political doctrine which called for a revolution of the common, working-class people and the establishment of a strong government which did not allow private ownership of businesses or property. Communism, like fascism, imposed strict control over every aspect of people's lives. After the Russian Revolution of 1917, this form of government came to power in Russia, which was renamed the Soviet Union (Union of Soviet Socialist Republics or U.S.S.R.).

These two political factions—fascism and communism—clashed violently in many countries and were fiercely debated even in the United States. The Spanish Civil War from 1936 to 1939 was a major battleground between these forces. The Spanish fascists ultimately won in 1939.

EUROPE DURING WORLD WAR II

Reading Passages

World War II: Causes *(cont.)*

Appeasement and Military Weakness

Another major cause of the Second World War was *appeasement*, the failure of the major powers to firmly and effectively halt the aggression of the Axis powers before the war. When Germany invaded Austria in 1938, the major powers merely accepted Hitler's control of that country. They agreed to Germany's takeover of the Sudetenland, an area of western Czechoslovakia with many German-speaking people, and then did nothing when Hitler invaded the rest of Czechoslovakia. The major powers did not stand up to Mussolini or the Japanese warlords either.

France, Poland, and most other countries—including the United States—did not have a strong, modern army and navy to counteract the massive military build-up in Germany and Japan. The Axis powers were armed and ready for war, but the Allied powers had few troops, out-of-date weapons and tactics, and ill-equipped soldiers.

Joseph Stalin

The War Begins

World War II officially began on September 1, 1939, when Germany invaded Poland. The governments of France and Great Britain honored treaty obligations and went to war in defense of Poland. Joseph Stalin, the dictator of the Soviet Union, and Hitler had signed a nonaggression pact. In the same month that Hitler invaded Poland from the West, Stalin's troops invaded Poland from the east. They divided the country between themselves. The Soviets then invaded Finland.

Germany Invades the West

In April 1940, German troops invaded Denmark and Norway. Neither of these countries was strong enough to offer much resistance. German divisions used their system of war called a *blitzkrieg*, or "lightning war." Massive numbers of German tanks and bombers overran and crippled military defenses in Denmark and Norway. Well-armed and highly-trained infantry troops then quickly destroyed any remaining opposition. In May, Germany invaded and conquered Belgium, the Netherlands, and most of France. From July through October of that year, Germany planned to invade and conquer England. German aircraft bombed British airfields, naval stations, and cities. Eventually, Hitler turned his attention east.

Reading Passages

World War II: The Fighting

German Forces Face East

In April 1941, German troops invaded Greece and Yugoslavia. In June 1941, in the most critical decision of the war, Hitler broke his non-aggression pact with Soviet ruler Joseph Stalin and attacked the Soviet Union. The Germans invaded deep into Russian territory where their armies met fierce resistance from the Soviet army and found their supply lines disrupted. German advances were finally halted by the Russians after terrible losses at Stalingrad. The Russians then began a gradual reconquest of their country and pushed the Germans back.

The U.S. Enters the War

On December 7, 1941, the Japanese government, convinced that the United States would eventually become involved in the war, launched a surprise attack on the U.S. naval base at Pearl Harbor in Hawaii with the intent of severely crippling America's military strength. The attack did severe damage to the U.S. fleet. The United States declared war on Japan the next day and shortly thereafter on Germany.

America—Arsenal of Democracy

Despite the losses at Pearl Harbor, the industrial capability of the United States was quickly mobilized. The U.S. quickly increased the size of its army and began overhauling its factories to manufacture weapons, ammunition, ships, planes, tanks, and the other necessities of war. In addition to supplying its own military, the United States was able to ship these products to its allies in Britain and the Soviet Union who were desperately in need of them. The United States was the "arsenal of democracy," supplying other countries as well as itself.

Fighting Back

In the Middle East, Allied troops gained control of Iraq, Syria, Lebanon, and Iran. In the battle of El Alamein in Egypt in 1942, they took command of Northern Africa. Allied troops invaded Italy, and Italy surrendered in 1943. In 1944 the Allies attacked German-held areas in Italy.

 Reading Passages

World War II: The Fighting *(cont.)*

D-Day at Normandy

On June 6, 1944, the Allies launched the greatest *amphibious* (land and water) assault in history at Normandy on the coast of France. More than 2,700 ships and 175,000 men participated in the invasion of Europe. After bitter fighting, the Allied forces of England, the United States, and French Freedom Fighters finally broke through stiff German resistance in late July 1944, rolled eastward liberating Paris in August, and pushed on toward Germany. German troops stopped the Allied advance temporarily at the Ardennes Forest in Belgium, but in the Battle of the Bulge, American and Allied troops eventually won and moved on toward Germany.

Soviets Push Germany Back

Soviet forces hammered German troops in the east. After the Soviet victory at the Battle of Stalingrad, their troops pushed steadily west. They won a massive tank battle at Kursk, forcing the Germans to retreat to save their remaining tanks. In January 1944, the Soviets ended a two-year German siege of Leningrad where over a million of their citizens had died. By 1944 the Soviets had forced German troops off its own territory and invaded Germany. Hitler committed suicide on April 30, 1945, and Germany surrendered unconditionally on May 7, 1945.

War in the Pacific

After Pearl Harbor, Japan launched a series of victorious assaults. They overran Thailand, Burma, Hong Kong, Malaya, Singapore, Indonesia, much of New Guinea, and the Philippines. They were within striking distance of Australia.

The United States was able to win two decisive victories in the Battle of Coral Sea in May 1942 and the crucial Battle of Midway in June 1942. This latter battle was probably the most important naval engagement in 500 years. It turned the tide of war for the U.S. and its allies. In a major series of battles, American troops and their allies retook the Gilbert, Marshall, and Mariana Islands, which became bases for launching air attacks against Japan itself. Allied forces invaded the Philippines and Burma.

The War Ends

On August 6, 1945, the United States dropped an atomic bomb on Hiroshima in Japan. Three days later they dropped a second bomb on Nagasaki. The effects of these bombs were devastating and caused enormous destruction and more than 100,000 casualties. On August 14, the Japanese surrendered, ending World War II.

Reading Passages

The Korean War

Prelude to War

In the late 1800s, Japan was a rising military and industrial power in the Far East. In 1895 it gained control of the Korean peninsula and formally annexed it to Japan in 1910. The defeat of Japan by the Allied forces in World War II forced the Japanese occupation forces to leave Korea. As a result, Soviet troops occupied the area of Korea north of the 38th parallel, and U.S. troops occupied the southern half of the peninsula.

Causes of the War

The Korean War was a part of the wide-ranging conflict between the United States and the Soviet Union known as the *Cold War*. The United Nations (U.N.) had decided that elections should be held in 1947 throughout Korea to decide on a form of government for the country. In 1948 the people of South Korea elected their own government and established democratic institutions. The Soviet Union was unwilling to allow elections in North Korea and formed a puppet regime there. Despite clashes between North and South Korean troops along the border between the two countries, the United States withdrew its troops in 1949. This was interpreted as a lack of interest in this part of the world, which triggered the North Koreans and their communist sponsors—the Soviet Union and China—to attack South Korea.

The Conflict Begins

Troops from communist North Korea invaded South Korea on June 25, 1950. The United Nations called the invasion a violation of international peace and demanded immediate withdrawal of the troops, but the North Koreans ignored these demands. The U.N. voted to take action and assist the South Koreans in their fight against the communist aggressors. Because the Soviet Union had been boycotting the U.N. over Nationalist China's membership in the U.N. Security Council, it was unable to veto the Security Council Resolution.

Forty-one countries sent aid, food, or military supplies to the South. With the support of Congress, President Harry Truman ordered U.S. forces into action on June 30 (although war was never officially declared). Eventually, the United States provided about 90% of the troops and equipment used by the allies during the war. When the hostilities broke out, the North Korean army had about 135,000 soldiers, and the South Korean forces numbered about 95,000.

American Troops Arrive

U.S. troops landed south of the capital at Seoul and engaged North Korean troops on July 5. Seoul had already been captured by communist forces. Despite the arrival of a U.S. Marine brigade and the U.S. 2nd Infantry Division and other units in late July, the Allies were pushed to the southern tip of the Korean peninsula by August 2. They formed the Pusan Perimeter and fought intensely to prevent the total collapse of South Korea.

Reading Passages

The Korean War *(cont.)*

The Pusan Perimeter

The fighting at the Pusan Perimeter cost North Korea about 58,000 soldiers. In a series of battles, the American troops were able to reinforce their units, bring superior air power to bear, and fight the North Koreans to a draw. In mid-September 1950, General Douglas MacArthur, the supreme commander of the allied armed forces, planned and executed the landing of American forces at Inchon on the northwest coast of South Korea. The landing took North Korea by surprise. This immediately relieved pressure on the allied troops along the Pusan Perimeter by cutting off North Korean troops from their supply line. American troops then broke out of the Pusan line, inflicted heavy losses on the North Koreans, and moved north.

Allied Forces Invade North Korea

In October, South Korean and American forces invaded North Korea and captured several cities. Despite Chinese warnings to move back, MacArthur tried to push into the heart of North Korea and end the war. The Chinese attacked in far greater numbers than the Americans had anticipated and rapidly pushed them south—in the process splitting apart the two American commands. On December 4, 1950, some 20,000 U.S. Marines and other soldiers began a slow retreat from the Changjin Reservoir in North Korea called the "Frozen Chosun" to a port at Hungnam, where they were evacuated after a heroic and costly series of battles that held back part of the Chinese army.

Communist Counterattack

The Chinese and North Korean forces recaptured Seoul but were then pushed back by American troops led by General Matthew Ridgeway. The conflict gradually developed into a stalemate, a battle for the hills and other strategic positions along the 38th parallel. Truce talks began in July 1951 but continued inconclusively for two years while the armies jostled for position. In April 1951, President Truman removed General MacArthur from command because MacArthur had publicly advocated military options, including bombing part of China, which Truman and other leaders felt might lead to another world war.

General Douglas MacArthur

Truce

The most serious cause of the deadlocked peace talks was not the dividing line between North and South Korea, which would essentially follow the line of battle along the 38th parallel, but it was the question of voluntary *repatriation*, or return, of the soldiers involved in the fighting. Many soldiers fighting for the North Koreans and the Chinese did not want to return to their home countries, and the communist nations did not want to admit that some of its soldiers were unhappy. Peace was finally achieved in 1953 when Joseph Stalin, the communist ruler in the Soviet Union, died, and Dwight D. Eisenhower became the new American president.

Reading Passages

The Vietnam War

Beginnings

The Vietnam War was the longest war in which the United States was ever involved. U.S. participation began in 1957 and ended in 1975. However, this was really the second stage of a conflict which began in 1946. In the last decades of the 1800s, France had gained control of Indochina (the areas of Laos, Cambodia, and Vietnam) as part of its efforts to set up a colonial empire like England, Germany, and other European powers were doing. Japan conquered and controlled the region during World War II, but the defeat of Japan led to France's attempt to reestablish control over Indochina.

Ho Chi Minh

Ho Chi Minh, a dedicated nationalist, was a popular Vietnamese leader who had fought Japanese occupation. He wanted to unite Vietnam as a communist nation free from foreign occupation or domination. He and his Vietminh supporters fought an eight-year revolutionary war to free themselves from French colonial rule. They finally defeated the French army at Dien Bien Phu in a climactic battle that led to a peace treaty calling for free elections in 1956.

Two Vietnams

After the war, Minh established firm control of his Communist government in North Vietnam. He suppressed all other political parties, designed a system of land reform popular with the peasants, and established legal reforms giving women equality with men. The United States was fearful of the spread of communism into Vietnam and decided to support an anti-communist government in the South led by Ngo Dinh Diem, an autocratic leader who was anti-communist but not democratic. Diem and the United States refused to support popular elections in 1956 as agreed to by the peace treaty with France because Minh was popular and likely to win.

Diem tried to eliminate the Viet Cong (communist rebels who wanted to overthrow Diem and unify the country under Ho's rule). By 1960 the rebels appeared to be gaining strength, so U.S. President John F. Kennedy sent military advisors to support the unpopular South Vietnamese government.

Reading Passages

The Vietnam War *(cont.)*

Buddhist Opposition

Diem had been particularly heavy-handed and unfair in dealing with the Buddhists, who were a large majority of the South Vietnamese population. Several Buddhist monks set themselves on fire in protest, and this led to even greater resistance to the Diem government. A group of South Vietnamese generals overthrew Diem, which led to a series of unstable governments that came and went. North Vietnam took advantage of the turmoil and sent army units into the South. By 1964 the Viet Cong rebels and their northern supporters controlled about 75 percent of the population.

Gulf of Tonkin Resolution

A minor naval scuffle between North Vietnamese torpedo boats and two U.S. ships led to the Gulf of Tonkin Resolution passed by Congress. It was used by President Lyndon Johnson as the legal basis for increased military involvement in Vietnam. The United States was trying to prevent the fall of another country to communism. U.S. leaders were convinced of the *domino theory*—that the fall of one nation to communism made the fall of neighboring countries likely, just like dominoes falling in a row.

America Goes to War

In March 1965, President Johnson sent a unit of U.S. Marines to Vietnam. These were the first American combat ground troops in the war. The United States and North Vietnam both quickly increased their forces, and the war escalated rapidly. By 1965 the

United States had committed 65,000 troops to Vietnam, and by 1969, the United States had over 540,000 troops there. The South Vietnamese Army numbered about 800,000. Almost 70,000 other troops arrived from New Zealand, Australia, South Korea, Thailand, and the Philippines. North Vietnam and their Viet Cong allies had at least 300,000 troops.

President Lyndon Johnson

Strategies

The United States believed that it could use massive firepower and technological superiority to crush the rebellion as it had used them to defeat Germany and Japan. The U.S. launched an extensive bombing campaign in North Vietnam and sent planes to attack large troop formations. They effectively used their greater firepower on the ground in pitched battles against the North Vietnamese troops. Bombers attacked the enemy supply route known as the Ho Chi Minh trail through Laos, Cambodia, and Vietnam.

The Vietnam War (cont.)

War of Attrition

Sheer firepower, however, was not that effective against the hit-and-run guerrilla warfare tactics used by the Viet Cong and their allies, who fought a superb war of attrition by attacking and retreating before the Americans could react with useful counter measures. The lightly armed Viet Cong hid in the jungle terrain and fought very successfully using ambush attacks. They knew the land, had the support of some of the people, and could appear and vanish with ease.

Course of the War

From 1965 through 1967, the United States and its South Vietnamese allies fought the North Vietnamese and Viet Cong to a draw. The war was fought in hundreds of small villages and along thousands of jungle trails. The U.S. forces inflicted terrible casualties on the enemy armies and on the civilian population, but they were not able to force the withdrawal of the North Vietnamese or to win the hearts and minds of the South Vietnamese people.

Reaction in the United States

The massive cost in terms of the heavy American casualties led to increased resistance to the war as the United States kept sending more and more troops into the conflict. The financial cost of the war was also beginning to be felt as new taxes were imposed, and some of the social programs to help the poor were cut. The conflict between the *hawks* who supported the war and the *doves* who opposed the war led to large demonstrations and opposition to the military draft in the U.S.

The Tet Offensive

On January 30, 1968, the first day of the *Tet*, or Vietnamese New Year, North Vietnam launched a series of attacks against military bases as well as cities in South Vietnam, especially the capital city of Saigon and the ancient city of Hue. With the *Tet Offensive* they hoped to increase the American people's opposition to the war, cause uprisings in South Vietnamese cities, and defeat or cripple the military forces of the United States and South Vietnam.

The U.S. Changes Course

The North Vietnamese suffered huge casualties in the Tet Offensive, and they were unsuccessful in their military objectives. They did, however, cause the U.S. to reevaluate the war as many Americans became convinced that the war could not be won. As a result, President Johnson refused to send another 200,000 troops requested by American generals, and he cut back on the bombing of North Vietnam. Johnson also called for peace negotiations and decided not to seek reelection as president. Peace talks opened in May but were not successful.

Reading Passages

The Vietnam War *(cont.)*

Nixon Looks for an Exit Strategy

After his election in 1968, President Richard Nixon tried to reduce U.S. involvement in Vietnam by increasing the training of the South Vietnamese army and gradually withdrawing U.S. ground troops. The road to peace was littered with obstacles. The U.S. sent forces into Cambodia in April 1970 to destroy huge supplies of war material stockpiled by the North Vietnamese. This probably prevented another massive North Vietnamese attack.

The U.S. Senate voted to repeal the Gulf of Tonkin Resolution, which made it more difficult for the president to fund the war. Protests in American cities and on college campuses became larger and more violent, and four students were killed at Kent State University in Ohio in a clash with National Guardsmen. In 1971 Lieutenant William Calley was court-martialed and imprisoned for his role in the My Lai massacre of several hundred innocent Vietnamese civilians.

President Richard Nixon

The End of the War

In March 1972, North Vietnam began another major invasion into South Vietnam. The U.S. responded by bombing North Vietnam, its troops, and supplies. The invasion was stopped in the summer of 1972, and a new round of peace negotiations began. A cease-fire was signed in January of 1973 between all of the major parties in the conflict, and the last U.S. ground troops were withdrawn. No peace treaty was signed, however, and North Vietnam began a relentless series of attacks which culminated in the capture of Saigon on April 30, 1975. The war was finally over.

The Cost

More than 58,000 American soldiers were killed in the Vietnam conflict, and more than 300,000 were wounded. North Vietnamese forces lost one million dead and more than 600,000 wounded. South Vietnam suffered 224,000 military deaths, more than one million soldiers wounded, and as many as 10 million civilian refugees, although no one knows exactly how many Vietnamese civilians on both sides were killed or wounded. The country's agriculture and industrial capabilities were severely crippled for years to come.

Reading Passages

The Cold War

Uneasy Allies

The end of World War II saw the defeat of the Axis powers in Germany and Japan and brought freedom and hope to many nations and peoples who had been invaded and conquered by them. The end of the war also brought an end to the uneasy alliance which had been formed between the democratic Western allies (Great Britain, France, and the United States) and the communist Soviet Union (Union of Soviet Socialist Republics or U.S.S.R.). The two superpowers—the United States and the U.S.S.R.—became enemies in 1945 because their beliefs and objectives were completely at odds. This philosophical conflict between the two countries came to be known as the *Cold War.*

Soviet Areas of Influence

The United States and its democratic allies throughout the world were committed to the spread of democracy and self-rule among all nations, especially those nations liberated from *Nazi* oppression. (Nazis were members of Hitler's Nationalist Socialist German Worker's Party, which supported nationalism, militarism, and racism.) The Soviet Union, led by dictator Joseph Stalin, was determined to increase its territorial control and subject these nations to its own communist-controlled government.

In Europe the U.S.S.R. occupied Poland, Czechoslovakia, Hungary, Romania, Bulgaria, East Germany, Latvia, and Lithuania and encouraged a communist-controlled government in Yugoslavia. The Soviets increased their influence in Asia by supporting the communist takeover of China. Their efforts to expand communism and the Soviet Union's power were worldwide.

An Iron Curtain Comes Down

Winston Churchill, the great British war leader, declared that an "iron curtain" had come down between the democratic West and the communist Soviet empire in the East. The aggressive efforts of the Soviet Union were met by a policy of containment by the United States and its allies as they tried to keep communism from spreading to other nations. For the most part, the Cold War developed not as an actual shooting war but as a series of actions and reactions by each side as it tried to strengthen its position.

Winston Churchill

Armed to the Teeth

Both sides maintained strong armies, equipped with the most up-to-date weapons. Their navies were equipped with the best ships and most technologically advanced weapons and guidance systems. Their nuclear-powered submarines patrolled the oceans. Soviet and American air forces were stocked with cutting-edge military planes as each side sought to build the fastest and most destructive fleet of fighter jets.

Reading Passages

The Cold War *(cont.)*

Nuclear Weapons

The United States created the first atomic weapons as World War II came to an end. The only two atomic bombs ever used in warfare were dropped on the Japanese cities of Hiroshima and Nagasaki, bringing an end to the war. After the war, the United States and the Soviet Union began building and stockpiling nuclear weapons and the missiles and planes to deliver them.

The Soviets stole some of their technology from the U.S. and developed some on their own. Other major nations developed the technology also, and the *proliferation*, or rapid increase, of nuclear weapons became a major world concern. It became obvious that nuclear war was a serious risk to the entire planet since nations had stockpiles of materials that could destroy the world several times over. Intercontinental ballistic missiles (ICBMs) could carry nuclear destruction across the oceans in a matter of minutes.

Cold War Alliances

The United States and Western European nations established the North Atlantic Treaty Organization (NATO) to form a barrier and a strong support system against potential Soviet aggression. Other organizations were created with allies in Asia and the Pacific. Member nations pledged to go to war to prevent the U.S.S.R. and its allies from extending its influence by force.

The Soviets created the Warsaw Pact, an alliance of its satellite Eastern European nations including Poland, Czechoslovakia, and Romania, to oppose the United States and NATO. The Soviets sent troops into Czechoslovakia in 1956 and Hungary in 1968 when those nations threatened to create independent, more democratic governments.

War by Proxy

The United States and the Soviet Union did not directly go to war against each other, but they were often involved in conflicts involving other nations. American participation in the Korean War was an effort by the United States to prevent the spread of communism in Asia. The Vietnam War was an effort by the Soviet Union and China to expand their sphere of influence and the U.S. to contain the spread of communism. The Soviet war in Afghanistan was another effort to extend communist influence.

From the Brink of Nuclear War to Disarmament

In 1962 the Soviets built missile bases in Cuba, a Soviet ally and communist nation located just 90 miles from the United States. The U.S. sent ships to blockade Cuba until the missiles and bases were removed. For a few intense days, nuclear war seemed very possible until the situation was finally resolved peacefully.

In 1969 the U.S. and U.S.S.R. began disarmament discussions, and a series of proposals and treaties finally led to a reduction in nuclear weapons in the 1980s. The end of the Soviet Union came about in 1991, and with its fall came the end of the Cold War.

Reading Passages

Other 20th Century Conflicts

There were many smaller conflicts in the 20th century involving countries that were trying to conquer other nations or avoid being destroyed by their neighbors. Wars were caused by religious hatred, possession of ancient tribal lands, and efforts to achieve political power, wealth, or revenge.

Arab-Israeli Conflicts

The longstanding Arab-Israeli conflict reflects the efforts of two nationalist movements—the Arabs and the Jews—to control Palestine, an area of land both groups claim as their ancient homeland. The roots of the conflict in recent times go back to the early years of the 20th century when European Jews began settling in Palestine. The movement to acquire a Jewish homeland grew rapidly with the end of World War II. In 1947 the United Nations divided Palestine into an Arab state and a Jewish state.

In 1948 several Arab nations invaded the new Jewish state of Israel but did not defeat the Jews. Small wars were fought in 1956, 1967, and 1973. The Six-Day War in 1967 clearly established Israeli military superiority. Israeli forces destroyed the Arab air forces, and the Israeli army defeated the Arab armies. A cease-fire was arranged after six days. The conflict is ongoing with many Palestinian terrorist attacks and reprisals by Israeli forces.

The Persian Gulf War

The United States had a rocky relationship with the dictators who ruled Iraq since the 1960s. In August 1990, Saddam Hussein, the Iraqi president, invaded Kuwait in a dispute over oil production, Iraqi debts to Kuwait, and territory. The United States organized and led a United Nations-sponsored coalition of 39 nations to oust Iraqi troops from Kuwait.

War began on January 16, 1991, with massive aerial attacks from the coalition forces. On February 23, American troops began moving into Iraq and defeating the Iraqi army. After 100 hours of fighting, President George Bush called a halt to the fighting. Iraqi forces were expelled from Kuwait, and Hussein agreed to the conditions imposed by the United Nations. He did not actually live up to many of the agreements after the war, however.

The Iran-Iraq War

In September 1980, Saddam Hussein sent his army across the border into Iran, beginning a war that would last eight years. The dispute began because Iran was supporting Kurdish rebels and Shiite Muslims in Iraq. There were territorial disputes as well. Bombing by both sides disrupted the two country's economies, severely reduced oil production, and damaged roads, bridges, factories, homes, and power plants. Hundreds of thousands of civilians and soldiers on both sides were killed or injured. A cease-fire stopped the fighting in 1988 without a clear victor.

 Reading Passages

Other 20th Century Conflicts *(cont.)*

The Russo-Japanese War

Russian expansion into Manchuria, an area of China, in 1901 led to conflict with Japan which wanted to control the same area. In 1904, Japan attacked Port Arthur, a major Russian naval base in the south of Manchuria. After a long siege with a series of brutal, high-casualty assaults, Japan captured Port Arthur in January 1905. Then they drove the Russians out of Manchuria and totally destroyed the Russian navy in the Battle of Tsushima.

Meanwhile, at home, the Russian government was in turmoil due to rebellion, which made Russia agree to peace rather than continue fighting. U.S. President Theodore Roosevelt received the Nobel Peace Prize for negotiating an end to this war.

The Balkan Wars

The gradual decline of the Ottoman Empire in the 19th century led to the formation of small nations who wanted to be independent of the Ottoman Turks and of other great powers. These Baltic states included Greece, Bulgaria, Serbia, and Montenegro. In 1912 these states attacked Turkey and defeated it partly because Turkey was undergoing a revolution itself.

After this First Balkan War, Albania proclaimed its independence, and the great powers of Austria-Hungary and Russia vied to keep any one Balkan state from becoming too powerful. A Second Balkan War broke out between Bulgaria and its former allies in June 1913. Bulgaria was defeated, and Serbia made the most territorial gains which worried her neighbors, especially Austria-Hungary. These Balkan wars set the stage for World War I.

21st Century War

In March 2003, the United States led a coalition of other nations in a second war against Iraq. President George W. Bush and his administration believed that Saddam Hussein had a huge storehouse of weapons of mass destruction, was supporting terrorism, and was developing nuclear weapons. The Iraqi army was defeated within several weeks, but a long period of insurgency followed as the United States tried to help Iraq create a modern democratic state.

President George W. Bush

World War I: Early Stages Quiz

Directions: Read pages 8–10 about the early stages of World War I. Answer each question below by circling the correct answer.

1. Which country was never a member of the Triple Alliance?
   a. Germany
   b. Great Britain
   c. Austria-Hungary
   d. Italy

2. Which country did Germany invade in order to attack France along an unguarded border?
   a. Russia
   b. England
   c. Belgium
   d. Spain

3. What did European nations want from Asian and African colonies?
   a. wealth
   b. cheap manpower
   c. weapons
   d. both a and b

4. Which act by a nation was considered essentially an act of war?
   a. making alliances
   b. conquering colonies
   c. mobilizing an army
   d. remaining neutral

5. Whose assassination led directly to World War I?
   a. Archduke Franz Ferdinand
   b. Queen Victoria
   c. Kaiser Wilhelm II
   d. Woodrow Wilson

6. In what year did the United States enter World War I?
   a. 1918
   b. 1917
   c. 1914
   d. 1915

7. Which of these countries was not a major European power in 1914?
   a. France
   b. Belgium
   c. Austria-Hungary
   d. Germany

8. What is the name of a knife attached to the barrel of a rifle?
   a. hand grenade
   b. machine gun
   c. bayonet
   d. trench

9. Which of the following was not a characteristic of trench warfare?
   a. quick recovery of wounded
   b. mud, filth, and insects
   c. poisonous gas
   d. bayonet fights

10. What kind of gas was used in World War I against soldiers in the trenches?
    a. hydrogen and ammonia
    b. oxygen and hydroxide
    c. argon and dioxide
    d. chlorine and mustard

World War I: Later Stages Quiz

Directions: Read pages 11 and 12 about the later stages of World War I. Answer each question below by circling the correct answer.

1. In which battle did the French forces declare, "They shall not pass!"?
   a. Somme
   b. Verdun
   c. Marne
   d. Masurian Lakes

2. Which of these sites was the scene of a Russian defeat?
   a. Marne
   b. Tannenberg
   c. Masurian Lakes
   d. both b and c

3. Which army simply dissolved and quit fighting?
   a. German
   b. British
   c. Russian
   d. French

4. Who defeated the British forces on the Gallipoli Peninsula?
   a. Germany
   b. Turkey
   c. France
   d. Russia

5. Who was the tsar?
   a. Russia's ruler
   b. Germany's military leader
   c. Austria-Hungary's king
   d. France's secret police

6. How many troops did the United States send to fight in World War I?
   a. 1 million
   b. 200,000
   c. 2 million
   d. 21 million

7. About how many soldiers were killed in World War I?
   a. 5 million
   b. 10 million
   c. 2 million
   d. 40 million

8. When did the armistice take effect?
   a. November 1918
   b. June 1918
   c. April 1917
   d. November 1916

9. The peace treaty ending World War I tried to punish which country?
   a. United States
   b. France
   c. Russia
   d. Germany

10. In which battle did the British try to end the stalemate with Germany?
    a. Somme
    b. Marne
    c. Verdun
    d. Gallipoli

World War II: Causes Quiz

Directions: Read pages 13–15 about the causes of World War II. Answer each question below by circling the correct answer.

1. About how many soldiers were killed in World War II?
   a. 35 million
   b. 17 million
   c. 70 million
   d. 2 million

2. Which country was not an Axis power?
   a. Germany
   b. Italy
   c. Great Britain
   d. Japan

3. Which of these was not a cause of World War II?
   a. the Treaty of Versailles
   b. fascism
   c. dictatorships
   d. democracy

4. What is the name for a dictatorial national government?
   a. communism
   b. democracy
   c. depression
   d. fascism

5. About how many soldiers were involved in World War II?
   a. 70 million
   b. 17 million
   c. 7 million
   d. 35 million

6. Which kind of government did Russia have after the Russian Revolution?
   a. democracy
   b. communist
   c. monarchy
   d. fascist

7. What name did the Germans use for "lightning war"?
   a. blitzkrieg
   b. depression
   c. fascism
   d. trench warfare

8. Which country did Germany not invade in 1940?
   a. France
   b. Belgium
   c. Great Britain
   d. the Netherlands

9. Which country did Germany invade that started World War II?
   a. Czechoslovakia
   b. Austria
   c. France
   d. Poland

10. Which country was controlled by a small group of military officers?
    a. Japan
    b. Great Britain
    c. Germany
    d. France

World War II: The Fighting Quiz

Directions: Read pages 16 and 17 about the fighting and battles during World War II. Answer each question below by circling the correct answer

1. What country did Germany break a non-aggression pact with and attack?
   a. Soviet Union
   b. Italy
   c. Great Britain
   d. Poland

2. Where was the atomic bomb dropped?
   a. Pearl Harbor
   b. Hiroshima
   c. Nagasaki
   d. both b and c

3. When did Germany unconditionally surrender?
   a. May 7, 1945
   b. December 7, 1941
   c. August 14, 1947
   d. April 30, 1942

4. How many men participated in the D-Day landing at Normandy?
   a. 700
   b. 4,000
   c. 175,000
   d. 2 million

5. Which battle was probably the most important naval battle in 500 years?
   a. Battle of Coral Sea
   b. Invasion of Normandy
   c. Pearl Harbor
   d. Battle of Midway

6. Which battle was not a Soviet victory against the Germans?
   a. Stalingrad
   b. El Alamein
   c. Leningrad
   d. Kursk

7. Which Axis country surrendered in 1943?
   a. Germany
   b. Russia
   c. Italy
   d. Japan

8. Which country launched a surprise attack on the United States?
   a. Germany
   b. Japan
   c. Great Britain
   d. Italy

9. Which country became the "arsenal of democracy," shipping war supplies to its allies?
   a. Great Britain
   b. United States
   c. France
   d. Russia

10. Where was World War II fought?
    a. Europe
    b. Asia
    c. the Middle East
    d. all of the above

The Korean War Quiz

Directions: Read pages 18 and 19 about the Korean conflict. Answer each question below by circling the correct answer.

1. Which country was forced out of Korea after World War II?
   a. China
   b. Soviet Union
   c. the United States
   d. Japan

2. What country invaded South Korea?
   a. Germany
   b. Great Britain
   c. North Korea
   d. Australia

3. When did the Korean War take place?
   a. 1910–1912
   b. 1945–1948
   c. 1950–1953
   d. 1975–1981

4. Which country boycotted the U.N. debates during the North Korean invasion?
   a. North Korea
   b. Soviet Union
   c. the United States
   d. China

5. Where in South Korea did American and South Korean troops halt the advancing North Korean army?
   a. Pusan Perimeter
   b. Changjin Reservoir
   c. Seoul
   d. Inchon

6. What word refers to soldiers returning home?
   a. annex
   b. repatriation
   c. boycott
   d. regime

7. Which American officer was relieved of his command for publicly advocating the bombing of China?
   a. General Ridgeway
   b. General Eisenhower
   c. General MacArthur
   d. General Walker

8. Where was the final line of battle?
   a. 38th parallel
   b. Pusan Perimeter
   c. 32nd parallel
   d. Frozen Chosun

9. The Korean War was considered a . . .
   a. North Korean victory.
   b. South Korean victory.
   c. American victory.
   d. stalemate.

10. What leader's death helped end the Korean War?
    a. President Eisenhower
    b. Joseph Stalin
    c. General MacArthur
    d. President Truman

The Vietnam War Quiz

Directions: Read pages 20–23 about the Vietnam War. Answer each question below by circling the correct answer.

1. When did U.S. involvement in the Vietnam War begin?
   a. 1957
   b. 1946
   c. 1975
   d. 1980

2. Which South Vietnamese leader did the United States support?
   a. Ho Chi Minh
   b. Vietminh
   c. Viet Cong
   d. Ngo Dinh Diem

3. What were communist rebels who supported Ho Chi Minh called?
   a. Viet Cong
   b. zealots
   c. Buddhists
   d. North Vietnamese

4. What were supporters of the war called?
   a. hens
   b. hawks
   c. doves
   d. eagles

5. Which army used guerrilla warfare tactics effectively?
   a. the Viet Cong
   b. the United States
   c. South Vietnamese
   d. French

6. What term expresses the idea that the fall of one country to communism would lead to the fall of other nations?
   a. guerrilla warfare
   b. domino theory
   c. cease-fire
   d. escalation

7. How many wounded and dead did the U.S. have in Vietnam?
   a. 4,000
   b. 58,000
   c. 1 million
   d. 358,000

8. Which event caused the U.S. to reevaluate its role in Vietnam?
   a. Gulf of Tonkin Resolution
   b. Battle of Dien Bien Phu
   c. Tet Offensive
   d. My Lai massacre

9. Which U.S. president was not involved with the Vietnam War?
   a. John F. Kennedy
   b. Richard Nixon
   c. Ronald Reagan
   d. Lyndon Johnson

10. When did the war in Vietnam end?
    a. 1975
    b. 1963
    c. 1968
    d. 1989

The Cold War Quiz

Directions: Read pages 24 and 25 about the Cold War. Answer each question below by circling the correct answer.

1. Who first used the term "iron curtain" in a speech?
   a. Franklin Roosevelt
   b. Winston Churchill
   c. Harry Truman
   d. Joseph Stalin

2. What did the "iron curtain" divide?
   a. Russia and China
   b. the U.S. and Great Britain
   c. democracy and communism
   d. Germany and France

3. What word means "the rapid increase of"?
   a. alliance
   b. proliferation
   c. nuclear
   d. atomic

4. Which two superpowers became enemies in 1945 because their beliefs and objectives were at odds?
   a. Great Britain and France
   b. Germany and Japan
   c. United States and Cuba
   d. United States and Soviet Union

5. Which country was not occupied by the Soviet Union after World War II?
   a. Poland
   b. Czechoslovakia
   c. France
   d. Hungary

6. In what year did the Cold War end?
   a. 1991
   b. 1945
   c. 1969
   d. 1962

7. What event almost led to nuclear war?
   a. Cuban missile crisis
   b. Vietnam War
   c. war in Afghanistan
   d. Czechoslovakian crisis

8. Which word means "complete destruction"?
   a. technology
   b. annihilation
   c. stockpiling
   d. intercontinental

9. In which conflict did the U.S. and Soviet Union compete against each other without directly fighting each other?
   a. Vietnam War
   b. Korean War
   c. war in Afghanistan
   d. all of the above

10. What was the name of the alliance of the Soviet Union and its Eastern European satellite nations?
    a. Warsaw Pact
    b. NATO
    c. Iron Curtain
    d. Bulgaria

Other 20th Century Conflicts Quiz

Directions: Read pages 26 and 27 about other 20th century conflicts. Answer each question below by circling the correct answer.

1. Which conflict set the stage for World War I?
   a. Russo-Japanese War
   b. Six Day War
   c. Iran-Iraq War
   d. Balkan Wars

2. Which war was caused by Iraq' invasion of Kuwait?
   a. Iran-Iraq War
   b. Persian Gulf War
   c. Russo-Japanese War
   d. Six Day War

3. Who made the most territorial gains in the Second Balkan War?
   a. Bulgaria
   b. Albania
   c. Serbia
   d. Greece

4. What country did the Balkan states attack in the First Balkan War?
   a. Austria-Hungary
   b. Russia
   c. Germany
   d. Turkey

5. Where is Manchuria located?
   a. China
   b. Japan
   c. Russia
   d. Turkey

6. Who fought the Russo-Japanese War?
   a. Russia and Manchuria
   b. Russia and Japan
   c. China and Japan
   d. the U.S. and Japan

7. Who fought the Six-Day War in 1967?
   a. Israel and several Arab powers
   b. Egypt and Iran
   c. Japan and Russia
   d. the U.S. and Germany

8. Who won the Six-Day War?
   a. Egypt
   b. the Arabs
   c. Israel
   d. Iran

9. What is a *coalition*?
   a. an alliance of nations
   b. a war
   c. a conflict
   d. a type of bomb

10. Who was the Iraqi leader in the Persian Gulf and Iran-Iraq Wars?
    a. George Bush
    b. Saddam Hussein
    c. Joseph Stalin
    d. King Jordan

Teacher Lesson Plans for Language Arts

Vocabulary

Objective: Students will apply their language arts skills in vocabulary enrichment.

Materials: copies of Weapons of War (page 39) and Military Lingo (page 40); pictures of military weapons from books, encyclopedias, or the Internet

Procedure

1. Reproduce and distribute the Weapons of War and Military Lingo activity sheets. Review the terms, pronunciation, and definitions if necessary.

2. Display pictures of weapons for students to see. Have students complete the pages independently.

Assessment: Correct the vocabulary activity sheets together.

Letter Writing

Objective: Students will apply their language arts skills in writing a friendly letter.

Materials: copies of Letters Home (page 41); reference sources such as the Internet, textbooks, war stories, and movies

Procedure

1. Reproduce and distribute the Letters Home page. Review the assignment and the format of a friendly letter.

2. Tell students to use what they have learned in their reading to help write a letter.

Assessment: Allow students to share their letters with the class. Check that students used the correct format for a friendly letter.

Newspapers

Objective: Students will learn to find information in newspapers.

Materials: copies of Read All About It! (page 42) and newspapers

Procedure

1. Reproduce and distribute the Read All About It! activity sheet.

2. Hand out copies of newspapers. Review the sections in a newspaper and the types of information found there.

3. Have students complete the activity sheet independently or with a partner.

Assessment: Have students share their newspaper entries in small groups or with the class.

Teacher Lesson Plans for Language Arts *(cont.)*

Literature

Objectives: Students will read and respond to a variety of fiction and nonfiction books related to 20th century wars.

Materials: copies of *Letters from Rifka* (page 43); copies of *Number the Stars* (pages 44 and 45); copies of Focus on Author Lois Lowry (page 46); copies of Holocaust Literature (page 47); copies of War Diaries (pages 48 and 49); copies of *Farewell to Manzanar* (page 50); copies of *Sadako and the Thousand Paper Cranes* (page 51); copies of War Literature (pages 52 and 53); copies of the books *Number the Stars, Farewell to Manzanar, Letters from Rifka,* and *Sadako and the Thousand Paper Cranes*; plus copies of other books by Lois Lowry (see page 46), Holocaust books (see page 47), war diaries (see page 48), and war novels (see page 52)

Procedure

- Reproduce and distribute the *Letters from Rifka* activity sheet. Depending on the number of available books, assign the book to an individual, a small group, or the class to read. Have students answer the comprehension questions independently. As a class, review the discussion questions.

- Reproduce and distribute the *Number the Stars* activity sheets. Have students read the book independently, in small groups, or as a class. Have students answer the comprehension questions independently. In small groups or as a class, have them share their responses to the discussion questions. Have students complete the word search independently.

- Reproduce and distribute the Focus on Author Lois Lowry page. Have students read one of her books and write a brief report on it.

- Reproduce and distribute the Holocaust Literature page. Have students read one of the books and write a brief report on it.

- Reproduce and distribute the War Diaries activity pages. Have students read a war diary independently, in small groups, or as a class. Instruct them to complete the diary evaluation. As an extension, have them start a personal diary.

- Reproduce and distribute the *Farewell to Manzanar* activity sheet. Have students read the book independently, in a small group, or with the class. Have students answer the comprehension questions independently. As a class, discuss students' responses. Then, review the discussion questions together.

- Reproduce and distribute the *Sadako and the Thousand Paper Cranes* activity sheet. Have students answer the comprehension questions independently. In small groups or as a class, have them share their responses to the discussion questions.

- Reproduce and distribute the War Literature activity sheets. Have students choose a novel to read. Review the story outline with the class, and instruct the students to complete it after reading their book.

Assessment: Use the student activity pages and class discussions to assess students' understanding and performance on the literature selections.

Teacher Lesson Plans for Language Arts *(cont.)*

Speeches

Objective: Students will develop oral presentation skills and techniques for public speaking.

Materials: copies of Great Speeches (pages 54 and 55); copies of speeches listed on page 54 (available in books and on the Internet) and a recording of them if possible; additional speeches from books and Internet sources

Procedure

1. Ask students who they have heard give a speech in person or on television and what qualities a good public speaker needs to have (*personable, interesting, speaks clearly, etc.*).
2. Distribute the Great Speeches activity sheets. As a class, read and discuss the three speeches on page 54. If possible, listen to a recording of one or more of these speeches.
3. Have students complete the assignment independently.
4. As an extension, students can select a famous speech from this time period and deliver it or a portion of it to the class. Review with them the Tips for Giving a Speech on page 55.

Assessment: Assess students' understanding of the three political leaders' speeches by reviewing their answers to the assignment. Critique students' delivery of the speeches to the class.

Poetry

Objective: Students will write a cinquain poem about war.

Materials: copies of Poetry of War (page 56)

Procedure

1. Distribute the Poetry of War activity sheet. Discuss how to write a cinquain poem.
2. Have students complete the assignment independently. Allow them to share their poems with the class.

Assessment: Critique students' poems and use of expressive words.

Readers' Theater

Objective: Students will learn to present a dramatic reading.

Materials: copies of Readers' Theater Notes (page 57); copies of Readers' Theater: On Omaha Beach (pages 58 and 59); copies of Readers' Theater: Crystal Night (pages 60 and 61)

Procedure

1. Reproduce and distribute the Readers' Theater Notes. Review the basic concept of Readers' Theater with the class.
2. Reproduce and distribute Readers' Theater: On Omaha Beach and Readers' Theater: Crystal Night. Assign students to small groups, and give them several days to practice reading the script together.
3. Schedule class performances, and have students share their prepared scripts.
4. As an extension, have students use the suggestions on the bottom of page 57 to write their own readers' theater. Then have them present their plays to the class.

Assessment: Base performance assessments on pacing, volume, expression, and focus of the participants. Student-created scripts should demonstrate general writing skills, dramatic tension, and a good plot.

Weapons of War

Weapons

aircraft carrier	destroyer	radar
bayonet	hand grenade	sonar
bazooka	jet fighter	submarine
bomber	machine gun	tank
depth charge	land mine	torpedo

Directions: Match each weapon listed above with its description and use below.

_____ 1. an armored vehicle with guns and tractor treads that is used to attack infantry troops

_____ 2. an underwater ship armed with torpedoes and used to attack surface ships

_____ 3. an explosive bomb hidden under dirt and used to make an area dangerous to move in

_____ 4. a small, fast warship used to attack other ships

_____ 5. an airplane used to drop bombs on enemy targets

_____ 6. an airplane used to attack other planes

_____ 7. a rapid-firing weapon used to protect troops during an attack

_____ 8. a knife attached to a rifle that is used in hand-to-hand combat

_____ 9. an underwater explosive device used to attack submarines

_____ 10. an underwater missile used by submarines to attack other ships

_____ 11. a weapon with a long metal tube used to fire armor-piercing rockets

_____ 12. a small explosive carried by a soldier and used to throw at attackers

_____ 13. a large ship used to carry planes

_____ 14. a radio detecting and ranging system used to locate aircraft

_____ 15. a sound navigation and ranging system used to find underwater objects like submarines

Military Lingo

Directions: Match the military lingo in Column 1 with its meaning in Column 2.

Column 1

_____ 1. A.W.O.L.

_____ 2. barracks

_____ 3. boot camp

_____ 4. C rations

_____ 5. chow

_____ 6. dog tags

_____ 7. G.I.

_____ 8. infantry

_____ 9. K.P.

_____ 10. M.A.S.H.

_____ 11. mess hall

_____ 12. motor pool

_____ 13. M.P.

_____ 14. officer

_____ 15. paratrooper

_____ 16. platoon

_____ 17. R&R

_____ 18. sack time

_____ 19. sniper

_____ 20. WAC

Column 2

a. Women's Army Corp.

b. foot soldiers

c. where military vehicles are kept

d. soldier trained to parachute into battle

e. a group of soldiers

f. a long-distance marksman

g. food

h. military person in command

i. sleep time

j. absent without leave

k. dining hall

l. ready-to-eat food for combat

m. kitchen police, help with meals

n. military identification tags

o. basic military training

p. buildings where soldiers live

q. "rest and recuperation," vacations for soldiers

r. "government issue," a soldier

s. mobile army surgical hospital

t. military police

Letters Home

Soldiers on the battlefields are lonely. The letters they write home are sometimes filled with the horrors they have seen, but more often talk about the people back home they miss—wives, children, parents, and friends. They are also likely to find humor in the ugly circumstances of war and will joke about the terrible food, the disagreeable weather, their superior officers, and the hardships they endure.

Assignment

Choose one of the following assignments and write a letter on a separate sheet of paper using the informal letter style shown at the bottom of this page. Use reference sources such as textbooks, the Internet, war stories, and movies to discover the conditions faced on the battlefield or at home during a 20th century conflict.

- Assume the identity of a soldier fighting in one of the 20th century wars or a nurse working in a battlefield hospital. Write a letter to a friend, your parents, a loved one, or a neighbor. Describe the daily conditions from a soldier's point of view. Describe some of the difficulties encountered, a battle experience, or daily life in the military such as the food, medical treatment, or general conditions. Tell who and what you miss from home.

- Assume the identity of a parent, friend, loved one, or neighbor and write to a soldier fighting in one 20th century war. Tell the soldier what is happening at home with the family, relate news of your local community, and describe efforts to help soldiers at war. Mention the shortages of food, gasoline, or other items. Express your feelings about the war, and mention any political and social events.

Extension

Find out how to write to American soldiers serving overseas. Write a letter to a soldier, and then mail it.

(Date)

Dear _____,

_____

_____

_____

_____

_____

_____

_____

Sincerely yours,

(Signature)

Read All About It!

Until the Vietnam War in the 1960s, people received most of their news about a war from newspapers. Even today with hundreds of cable television channels and radio stations to choose from, a lot of people still read a newspaper to get in-depth information about a war or other event.

Directions: Get a newspaper, and read an article in each section listed below. Write the headline of the article and give one fact you discovered in each section.

Name of Newspaper: _____ **Date:** _____

1. **The World**

   Headline: _____

   Fact: _____

2. **The Nation**

   Headline: _____

   Fact: _____

3. **State or Local News**

   Headline: _____

   Fact: _____

4. **Editorial/Opinion**

   Headline: _____

   Fact: _____

5. **Sports**

   Headline: _____

   Fact: _____

6. **Business**

   Headline: _____

   Fact: _____

Extension

1. What is in each of these sections?

   a. Classifieds: _____

   b. Obituaries: _____

2. Did you read about a war or conflict in any part of the world? (Tell where and who is involved in the fighting.) _____

   _____

   _____

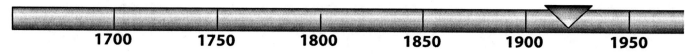

Letters from Rifka

Letters from Rifka by Karen Hesse tells the story of one family's efforts to escape the aftermath of World War I and the revolution in Russia. Told in the form of letters from a 12-year-old girl to her cousin still in Russia, the story chronicles the efforts of Rifka and her family to immigrate to America. The book is based on the true story of the author's aunt.

Comprehension Questions

Read *Letters from Rifka*. Then answer the following questions on a separate sheet of paper.

1. How did Rifka cost her parents a lot of money when she bought the orange?

2. Who is Rifka's favorite brother? Why?

3. How do Rifka's experiences change her attitude toward her family?

4. Where is Rifka writing her letters?

5. What is Rifka's special talent?

6. What kind of jobs did Rifka's parents get?

7. Why did Rifka's parents decide to leave Russia?

8. Why did Rifka's family leave her to distract the soldiers searching the train?

9. What was Rifka's most beautiful physical feature?

10. Who is Tovah?

Discussion Questions

Discuss the following questions with a small group or the entire class.

1. Why do you think the United States was so careful about admitting only healthy and able immigrants?

2. What was the attitude of the custom agents and the law toward a woman's value in society? Give examples from the story.

3. Why did the Russian peasants pick on the Jews?

4. What kind of a writer do you think Pushkin is? How does his writing relate to Rifka's story?

5. What is your personal attitude toward Saul?

6. How did Rifka's behavior create some of her problems? Give examples from the book.

7. Would you leave your child like Rifka's family did? Give your reasons.

8. How did diseases like typhus and ringworm affect people's lives in 1920?

9. What actions by Rifka demonstrate her character, courage, and kindness?

10. What is your favorite part of the book? Why?

Number the Stars

Number the Stars by Lois Lowry is the Newbery Award-winning novel of a Danish family trying to keep their Jewish friends from being deported, or sent away, by the Nazis. It is an extraordinary tale of courage and is based on real people and events.

Comprehension Questions

Read *Number the Stars*, including the Author's Note at the end of the book. Then answer the following questions on a separate sheet of paper.

1. Which girl in the story is the fastest runner?

2. Which girl is a talented actress?

3. Why does Kirsti hate her new shoes?

4. What are some of the shortages caused by the war?

5. How did Annemarie's dad convince the Nazis that Ellen was his daughter?

6. Why was it so important to get the packet to Uncle Henrik?

7. What was in the casket?

8. How did Annemarie's mother talk the German officer out of opening the casket?

9. What did the German guard dogs eat from Uncle Henrik's lunch?

10. What country did Ellen and her family go to for safety?

11. What did Annemarie save for Ellen until the war was over?

12. How did Ellen and her family escape from Denmark?

Discussion Questions

Discuss the following questions with a small group or the entire class.

1. Why do you think the young people in Denmark and other countries joined the Resistance Movement against the Nazis?

2. What are some of the dangers of living in a country occupied by foreign troops?

3. Why did the Danes resent the fact that the German soldiers did not speak their language well?

4. What hints do you have at the beginning of the book that Peter is involved in the Resistance?

5. What did the German soldiers and officials do that made the Danes angry?

6. Why do you think the Germans wanted to kill the Jews? What excuses did they use?

7. Why did Annemarie need to act like "an empty-headed little girl" when she met the German troops in the woods?

8. How does this book help you understand how people feel when they are occupied by any army—regardless of the reason?

Number the Stars *(cont.)*

The following words are used in the book *Number the Stars* to tell about the heroic rescue of the Jews in Denmark. Find these words in the wordsearch puzzle below.

channel	fishing boats	King Christian X	round up
coast	Germany	Nazis	sabotage
courage	Hitler	neutral	smuggle
death camps	Holocaust	rescue	Sweden
Denmark	Jews	resistance	villages

```
G  S  B  S  V  H  R  H  F  P  L  D  C  F  J  B  V  V  G  C  M  R  F  S
E  S  Y  H  A  N  N  B  L  B  C  K  Q  B  M  L  C  N  Y  J  E  R  Y  K
R  G  F  H  C  B  F  F  X  N  H  L  C  V  Z  J  Q  N  G  S  B  T  R  S
C  O  A  S  T  A  O  B  G  N  I  H  S  I  F  N  A  Z  I  S  E  A  S  R
N  Q  W  R  W  C  T  B  H  A  M  O  T  G  M  M  S  G  U  M  P  V  D
L  E  L  V  U  E  R  S  A  N  U  I  H  L  R  P  T  N  C  N  M  R  G  K
J  P  S  P  I  O  D  V  N  G  Z  V  T  E  O  A  M  S  E  A  L  C  P  F
G  H  B  Z  W  L  C  E  G  R  E  B  G  S  N  C  E  D  C  U  Y  J  W  V
R  D  I  B  B  L  L  L  N  P  O  J  J  C  I  R  A  H  K  Z  T  B  R  W
T  B  B  T  K  W  E  A  S  N  G  U  E  S  B  R  T  U  F  K  T  R  B  P
D  X  P  V  L  X  X  R  G  W  Z  V  N  Y  D  A  H  V  S  G  Q  F  A  R
F  J  K  W  G  E  S  R  X  E  G  Z  Y  D  E  L  T  C  R  T  X  R  L  L
V  S  D  T  Y  S  R  N  N  K  S  J  V  D  U  S  Y  B  G  X  H  G  Y  Q
C  M  W  G  M  G  Y  B  H  P  T  S  G  Z  V  P  S  N  H  N  S  X  T  M
Z  S  H  F  G  W  K  J  T  G  N  V  T  W  S  Y  B  F  Q  L  I  F  Z  C
J  S  W  F  L  C  T  B  W  F  W  R  W  T  M  F  H  V  P  Z  Y  K  H  J
```

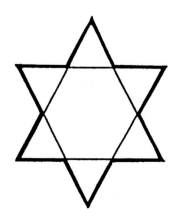

Focus on Author Lois Lowry

Lois Lowry was born on March 10, 1937, to an Army dentist and his wife. The middle of three children, Lois was a solitary child who loved to read and write poetry. She traveled to many parts of the world with her family and experienced cultures as different as Japan and the Amish countryside in Pennsylvania where her mother was raised. She attended college for two years before her marriage. She later finished college and began writing as her four children grew up. She published her first children's novel at the age of 40 and has been writing ever since.

Much of what Lowry writes flows out of her own experiences. Her first book, *A Summer to Die*, is a fictional account of her sister's death in her twenties. She wrote the book *The Giver* after watching her father lose his long-term memory to disease. The *Anastasia* series she wrote grew out of her family's life. Anastasia is a composite of her two daughters who are both outgoing, active, and very independent. Some of the events in the stories are based on things her girls actually did.

Lowry's book *Number the Stars* is based on the many stories she heard from her friend Annelise Platt, who as a child lived in Copenhagen, Denmark, during the German occupation of that country. Real historical events are woven into the story. These include the Danes sinking their ships in order to avoid surrendering their navy to the Germans, King Christian riding daily through the city of Copenhagen without guards, and the Danes using cocaine mixed with rabbit's blood to confuse the German dogs searching for Jews.

Assignment

Choose one of Lois Lowry's novels to read. Write a brief report on the novel for your reading group. Include a summary of the plot, a description of the main characters, and the theme of the book.

Anastasia Krupnik. Houghton, 1979. (This book and the Anastasia and Sam sequels are easy-to-read, humorous stories featuring a very intelligent girl with an independent nature.)

Gathering Blue. Houghton, 1996. (Kira is a handicapped child in this futuristic novel where each person must justify his value to the community. This story will make you think about the value of life.)

The Giver. Houghton, 1993. (This novel is about a society where people are controlled by a rigid set of rules from birth to death. It is haunting and very thought-provoking.)

The Silent Boy. Houghton, 2003. (This book deals with an autistic boy in the years before autism was understood or treated.)

A Summer to Die. Houghton, 1977. (This tells the story of a young girl's death.)

Holocaust Literature

The *Holocaust* is the term used to describe the efforts of the Nazi leaders in Germany to wipe out the Jewish people. More than six million Jews were killed, most of them in the slave-labor concentration camps run by the German government. This genocide, or deliberate and organized killing of people because of their race, religion, or political group, has been the subject of many books.

Assignment

Read one of the following books about the Holocaust or another of your choosing. Write a short book report that includes the plot, main characters, and your personal opinion of the book.

Books About the Holocaust

Drucker, Malka and Michael Halperin. *Jacob's Rescue: A Holocaust Story.* Bantam, 1993. (Based on a true story, eight-year-old Jacob is a Jew confined with his aunt to a Polish ghetto surrounded by Nazi troops. He slips out of the ghetto to live with a non-Jewish man, who risks his life and family to save the boy.)

Drucker, Olga Levy. *Kinderstransport.* Holt, 1992. (This is the autobiography of a Jewish girl sent from Germany to England in 1938 by her parents, who recognized the increasing danger for Jews in Germany. The story describes her years in England and her emigration to America.)

Matas, Carol. *Daniel's Story.* (In this first-person story, a 14-year-old boy is forced into a Jewish ghetto, separated from his family, and then sent to the Nazi death camp at Auschwitz.)

Pressler, Mirjam. *Malka.* Philomel, 2003. (While fleeing from Poland to avoid capture by the Germans, a young Jewish girl is separated from her mother and sister. Malka's life on the run in and near a Jewish ghetto in Poland is astonishing. This novel is based on a true story.)

Reiss, Johanna. *The Upstairs Room.* Crowell, 1972. (This is the exciting story of Annie and Sini, two young Jewish girls hiding in a Dutch farmer's home and confined to a single room for two years during the German occupation of Holland. It is based on the author's own experiences.)

Reiss, Johanna. *The Journey Back.* Crowell, 1976. (In this sequel to Reiss' book *The Upstairs Room*, the war is over and the family is trying to put their lives back together.)

Yolen, Jane. *The Devil's Arithmetic.* Viking, 1988. (This is the powerful story of a girl who is transported back in time to Nazi Germany during the Holocaust where she and her relatives are arrested and sent to a concentration camp.)

War Diaries

The most famous war diary of the 20th century is *The Diary of Anne Frank*, which chronicles the hopes and fears of a 13-year-old Jewish girl hiding with her family in a small annex in an old office building in Amsterdam, Holland. Some other diaries have been written for children to recreate the lives of people caught up in war.

Assignment

Read one of the diaries described below. Complete the evaluation on page 49. Give examples from the book to document your evaluation. Share what you learn with a small group or the entire class.

Nonfiction Diaries

Frank, Anne. *The Diary of a Young Girl*. Doubleday, 1967. (This teenage Jewish girl's diary was found after the war and originally published in 1952.)

Filipovic, Zlata. *Zlata's Diary: A Child's Life in Sarajevo*. Viking, 1994. (This is an extraordinary diary of an 11-year-old girl caught in the murderous civil war between the Bosnians and Serbs. It vividly details the hardships and tragedies of war.)

Fictional Diaries

Osborne, Mary Pope. *My Secret War: The World War II Diary of Madeline Beck*. Dear America Series, Scholastic, 2000. (This is the story of a girl in Long Island, New York, whose father is a sailor on duty in the Pacific. She lives near the ocean and tries to spot enemy ships and agents.)

Denenberg, Barry. *The Journal of Ben Uchida: Citizen 13559 Mirror Lake Internment Camp*. My Name is America Series, Scholastic, 1999. (This fictional account of a young boy's years at an internment camp was based on real events in the lives of many Japanese-Americans confined in relocation camps in the U.S.)

Myers, Walter Dean. *The Journal of Scott Pendleton Collins: A World War II Soldier*. My Name is America Series, Scholastic, 1999. (A 17-year-old soldier in the heat of combat in France records his fears, thoughts, and hopes in a journal.)

War Diaries *(cont.)*

Directions: Use this form as a guide to tell about the diary you read. Write your responses on a separate sheet of paper.

Diary Evaluation

Name of Diary

Person who wrote the diary
   Gender and age:
   Personality/character traits (outgoing, depressed, fearful, daring, proud, humble, defiant):
   Hopes and desires:

Setting
   Time
   Place

Circumstances/situation (battles, dangers, central problem facing the diarist):

Conflict (who and what does the diarist contend with):

Important characters in the diary (Give a brief description of each.)
   Friends
   Family
   Enemies

Events
   Describe one interesting event
   Describe one sad event
   Describe one happy event

Impressions (Tell your impressions of the diary.)

Extension

Start your own diary or journal today. Try to record at least one entry each day. Use the following ideas to help you think of what to write.

- Describe important events that are happening in your personal life.
- Tell about local, state, or world events that are affecting your life or that interest you.
- Describe books you are reading which influence your thinking.
- Mention some of your hopes, dreams, and plans for the future.
- Describe important people in your life.

Farewell to Manzanar

Because of concerns over the loyalty of Japanese-Americans after the Japanese bombed Pearl Harbor in 1941, the U.S. War Department relocated 110,000 Americans of Japanese ancestry living on the West Coast to 10 inland camps. *Farewell to Manzanar* by Jeanne Wakatsuki Houston and James Houston is a memoir of one Japanese-American child's experiences in Manzanar, a relocation camp in Owens Valley, California, during World War II.

Comprehension Questions

Read *Farewell to Manzanar*. Then answer the following questions on a separate sheet of paper.

1. When did Jeanne and her family get sent to Manzanar?

2. Who were the Issei?

3. Who was accused of being an "inu," or collaborator, with the Americans?

4. What is Papa's answer when he is asked whether he supports Japan or America during the war?

5. What does Jeanne do at Manzanar?

6. How does Papa feel about Jeanne becoming a Catholic?

7. How did the 442nd Regimental Combat Team distinguish itself?

8. What did Woody visit in Japan?

9. What skill is Jeanne especially good at which helps her make friends in junior high school?

10. Who is Radine?

Discussion Questions

Discuss the following questions with a small group or the entire class.

1. Why did Papa burn his Japanese flag?

2. Why were most Japanese living in the United States not American citizens?

3. Were Japanese living in America treated less fairly than immigrants from other nations? Give your reasons.

4. Were the relocation camps a reasonable precaution for Americans to take after the attack on Pearl Harbor? Explain your position.

5. How were the Japanese-Americans cheated by the relocation? Give several examples.

6. Describe Papa's personality and his work experiences.

7. How did Papa's samurai heritage in Japan affect his behavior in America?

8. What do you think was the most difficult part of living at Manzanar? Explain.

9. Why do you think Papa got drunk?

10. Why is it hard for Jeanne to be socially accepted in junior high and high school?

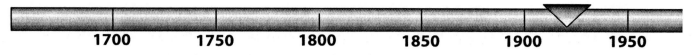

Sadako and the Thousand Paper Cranes

Sadako and the Thousand Paper Cranes by Eleanor Coerr is the story of a 12-year-old girl, Sadako Sasaki, who died as a result of the radiation she was exposed to when the atomic bomb was dropped on Hiroshima.

Comprehension Questions

Read *Sadako and the Thousand Paper Cranes*. Then answer the following questions on a separate sheet of paper.

1. What information does the book's prologue tell you?
2. Who was Oba Chan?
3. Who is Chizuko?
4. What does Sadako practice every day?
5. What disease did the doctors discover Sadako had?
6. What is the legend of the cranes?
7. Who is Kenji?
8. How many cranes did Sadako make?
9. On what day did Sadako die?
10. How many cranes did Sadako's classmates make after her death?

Discussion Questions

Discuss the following questions with a small group or the entire class.

1. Why did Sadako's mother make her the special kimono?
2. What is Sadako like?
3. How do you know that the Sasaki family is poor? Give clues from the story.
4. How do you know that Sadako is rather clumsy? Give examples from the story.
5. Why do you think it was good for Sadako to make the cranes?
6. What can you learn from the story about the unintended consequences of war?
7. Why do you think Peace Day is celebrated on August 6 in Japan?
8. Why do you think Sadako could remember the Thunderbolt (the atomic blast) even though she was only two at the time?
9. How would you feel and what would you do if you were Sadako lying in a bed in a hospital?
10. How do you know that many families were affected by the bomb?

War Literature

Assignment

The settings of many young adult books have been during one of the wars or military conflicts in the 20th century. Listed below are some of these novels. Read the brief descriptions, and choose a book which interests you. Read the book and then complete the story outline on page 53. Share what you learned with a small group or the entire class.

Books Set in Wartime

Choi, Sook Nyul. *Echoes of the White Giraffe*. Dell, 1993. (The sequel to *Year of Impossible Goodbyes*, a young girl gets separated from her family and becomes a refugee in the Pusan Perimeter during the Korean War.)

Choi, Sook Nyul. *Year of Impossible Goodbyes*. Dell, 1991. (This story tells of one North Korean family's battles against Japanese conquerors and Russian invaders and of their journey south to freedom. It is based on the author's own life.)

Forsyth, Frederick. *The Shepherd*. Viking, 1976. (The ghost of a legendary British pilot guides a lost pilot to safety through the fog over the English Channel.)

Garrigue, Sheila. *The Eternal Spring of Mr. Ito*. Bradbury, 1985. (This story is about an English girl sent to Canada for safety and the friendship she forms with a Japanese gardener despite Pearl Harbor, racial distrust, and internment camps.)

Giff, Patricia Reilly. *Lily's Crossing*. Delacorte, 1997. (Set during World War II, this is the story of an American girl whose father is fighting in Europe and the enduring friendship Lily forms with Albert, a war refugee.)

Greene, Bette. *Summer of My German Soldier*. Dell, 1973. (A 12-year-old Jewish girl living in a small Arkansas town befriends a German prisoner who escaped from a nearby detention center. This novel explores the limits of friendship and love.)

Hahn, Mary Downing. *Stepping on the Cracks*. Clarion, 1991. (Two American girls, whose older brothers are in Europe fighting Hitler's Germany, try to deal with an abused and abusive bully.)

Ho, Minfong. *The Clay Marble*. Farrar, 1991. (This is the story of a Cambodian family trying to escape the violence in their country. It highlights the value of faith and true friendship.)

Salisbury, Graham. *Under the Blood-Red Sun*. Dell, 1994. (A Japanese-American boy lives in Hawaii when Pearl Harbor is attacked. He, his family, and his baseball buddies try to retain some normalcy in a world at war.)

Whelan, Gloria. *Goodbye, Vietnam*. Delacorte, 1992. (Mai and her family are refugees who flee Vietnam, cross the South China Sea on a rickety boat, find themselves unwanted in Hong Kong, and eventually reach their goal of a new life in America.)

Wolff, Virginia Euwer. *Bat 6*. Scholastic, 1998. (This is a sports story built around the conflict between two girls on different softball teams representing two small Oregon towns. Shazam is a poor, nearly illiterate girl whose father was killed at Pearl Harbor. Aki is a Japanese girl recently returned from an internment camp.)

War Literature *(cont.)*

Story Outline

Genre (historical fiction, fantasy): _____

Setting of the novel (where and when): _____

Protagonist (one or two facts about the central character): _____

_____

Major Characters (1–2 descriptive facts about each): _____

_____

Lesser Characters (1–2 descriptive facts about each): _____

_____

Point of View (Is the novel told in first person or third person?): _____

_____

Plot (4–6 sentences giving the story line): _____

_____

_____

_____

Problem/Conflict (the basic problem in one sentence): _____

_____

Resolution (how the novel ends): _____

Feeling/Tone (book's general tone—uplifting, sad, funny, etc.): _____

Theme (novel's main idea): _____

_____

_____

Personal Evaluation (your response to the novel): _____

_____

Great Speeches

Many leaders in the 20th century were known for their ability to communicate. The following are excerpts from some famous speeches during this century.

"The world must be made safe for democracy. Its peace must be planted upon the tested foundations of political liberty. We have no selfish ends to serve. We desire no conquest, no dominion, We seek no indemnities for ourselves, no material compensation for the sacrifices we shall freely make. We are but one of the champions of the rights of mankind. We shall be satisfied when those rights have been made as secure as the faith and the freedom of nations can make them."

Woodrow Wilson on April 2, 1917

"I expect that the Battle of Britain is about to begin. Upon this battle depends the survival of Christian civilization. Upon it depends our own British life and the long continuity of our institutions and our Empire. The whole fury and might of the enemy must very soon be turned on us now. Hitler knows that he will have to break us in this island or lose the war. If we can stand up to him, all Europe may be free and the life of the world may move forward into broad, sunlit uplands. But if we fail, then the whole world, including the United States, including all that we have known and cared for, will sink into the abyss of a new Dark Age . . ."

Winston Churchill on June 18, 1940

". . . Yesterday, December 7, 1941—a date which will live in infamy—the United States was suddenly and deliberately attacked by naval and air forces of the empire of Japan . . . I ask that the Congress declare that since the unprovoked and dastardly attack by Japan on Sunday, December 7, 1941, a state of war has existed between the United States and the Japanese Empire,"

Franklin D. Roosevelt on December 8, 1941

Assignment

Answer the following questions on a separate sheet of paper.

1. What was happening when each of the speeches above was given?

2. What was the speaker's purpose in giving the speech? Who was the speaker trying to influence?

3. What was the main idea of the speech?

4. How effective do you think the speech was?

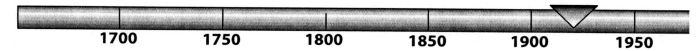

Great Speeches *(cont.)*

Extension

1. Choose one of the following speeches or find another 20th century speech on the Internet, in a book, or other source. Select a part of the speech or the entire speech if it is less than five minutes long.

   - Woodrow Wilson's The World Must Be Made Safe for Democracy speech

   - Winston Churchill's We Shall Never Surrender address

   - Franklin D. Roosevelt's Day of Infamy speech

   - Winston Churchill's Iron Curtain speech

   - Winston Churchill's Hush Over Europe radio broadcast

   - Hawaii Senator Daniel Inouye's 50th anniversary address to the 442nd Infantry Regimental Combat Team

2. Memorize the speech, or learn it very well. Try to get the tone and emphasis that the original speaker might have used.

3. Use the tips below to help you prepare, and then deliver your speech to the class.

Tips for Giving a Speech

☐ **Good Posture**—Stand up straight. Relax and try to be comfortable.

☐ **Use notes**—Type or neatly copy your speech on a piece of paper. Refer to the written speech when necessary, but do not just read the speech.

☐ **Eye Contact**—Look at the audience as you speak but not at any one person in particular.

☐ **Volume**—Change your voice to fit what is being said. Use a normal tone of voice for the most part, but emphasize important points. Speak loudly enough for your audience to hear you, but do not shout.

☐ **Pause**—Take deep breaths between paragraphs and at important points, but do not be too obvious about it. Often a short pause can be used effectively to emphasize a word or phrase.

☐ **Speak slowly and clearly**—Speak a little slower than normal. Do not rush through the speech or be in a hurry to finish. Pronounce words clearly so that everyone can understand what is being said.

☐ **Rehearse, rehearse, rehearse**—Say your speech out loud in front of a mirror, friend, sibling, or adult family member. Practice it several times so that you become familiar with what you are saying.

☐ **Enjoy the experience**—Public speaking is a great accomplishment. Take pride in being able to stand in front of an audience and give a short talk.

Poetry of War

Poetry is a style of writing that can bring thoughts and feelings to life through colorful words and verbal images. A cinquain is a five-line poem as shown below.

Line 1:	Title	1 word
Line 2:	Description of title	2 words
Line 3:	Action about the title	3 words
Line 4:	Feeling about the title	4 words
Line 5:	Synonym for the title	1 word

The following is an example of a cinquain written about war.

War

Leaving home

People dying daily

Can't stand the pain

Grief

Assignment

On the lines below, write a cinquain about war. Use words that express feelings and emotions and paint a picture in words about war.

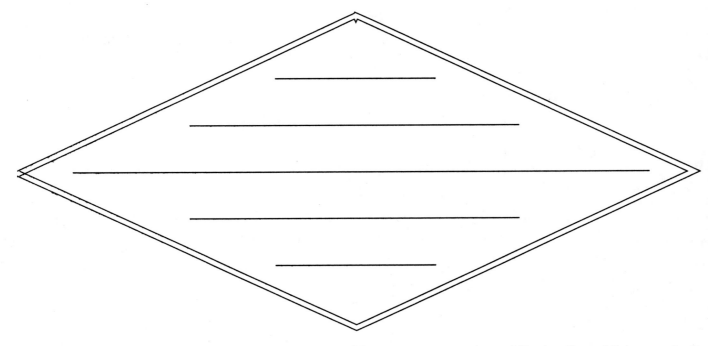

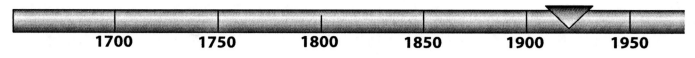

Readers' Theater Notes

Readers' Theater is drama without costumes, props, stage, or memorization. It is done in the classroom by groups of students who become the cast of the dramatic reading.

Staging

Place four or five stools, chairs, or desks in a semicircle at the front of the classroom or in a separate stage area. Generally no costumes are used in this type of dramatization, but students dressed in similar clothing or colors can add a nice effect. Props are unnecessary but can be used.

Scripting

Each member of the group should have a clearly marked, useable script. Practice several times before presenting the play to the class.

Performing

Performers should enter the classroom quietly and seriously. They should sit silently without moving and wait with their heads lowered. The first reader should begin, and the other readers should focus on whoever is reading, except when they are performing.

Assignment

1. Read the readers' theater script on pages 58 and 59 about the amphibious assault at Normandy and the script on pages 60 and 61 about the beginning of the Holocaust.

2. Choose one of the scripts, and practice it with a small group. Perform the play for the class.

Extension

Write your own readers' theater script based on one of the events listed below or another topic related to a conflict in the 20th century. Practice your script with a group of classmates, and then perform it for the rest of the class.

- A trench warfare skirmish or an effort to retrieve wounded soldiers during battle.

- Life in a Nazi concentration camp.

- Life in a Japanese relocation camp.

- A refugee escaping the terrors of war.

- A World War II battle scene such as Iwo Jima, a tank battle in Northern Africa, or the Battle of the Bulge.

- A scene for the home front during any war.

- A Vietnam War protest scene.

Readers' Theater: On Omaha Beach

Omaha Beach was the Allied codename for one of the main landing points during the Normandy landings on June 6, 1944. There are seven speaking parts in this script.

Narrator: This morning, June 6, 1944, the greatest amphibious assault in modern warfare is occurring on the beaches of Normandy along the coast of occupied France. A fleet of 2,700 ships and 176,000 troops from the United States, Great Britain, Canada, and France are beginning the liberation of Europe from the Nazi oppressors who have conquered and controlled most of the continent. As the scene begins, a squad of five American soldiers is waiting anxiously in a small landing craft moving slowly toward Omaha Beach.

Lieutenant: Men, we're 30 seconds from dropping the gangplank. Remember your training. If you wade too slowly through the water, you're going to be perfect targets for the German gunners on the hills overlooking the beach.

Private Scott: I'm scared.

Corporal: It's nothing to be ashamed of, Scott. We're all scared.

Sergeant: I tell you, Private, I've been through a lot of battles from the Kasserine Pass in Northern Africa to Sicily and up through Italy. They were terrible, but this is the worst I've ever seen. There are a lot of men dying out there.

Lieutenant: Go! Go! Go! Get to the beach!

Sergeant: Move out!

Private Scott: Help me! I'm hit. I'm hit in the chest!

Lieutenant: We got you kid. Hang on till we make the beach. Grab his other arm, Corporal.

Narrator: As the men struggle toward the shore, the firing from the hills overlooking the beach becomes more intense. Rifle, machine gun, and artillery fire fill the air, hitting the unprotected Allied soldiers. Soldiers are screaming in agony as they fall wounded in the water and on the beach. Some of those hit in the water drown. Others drown after being trampled by soldiers desperate to get onto the beach.

Sergeant: We're on the beach! Let's go. We've got to move inland. If we stay here, we die. There's no cover—no place to hide. We've got to go. Now! It's move out or die!

Lieutenant: My leg! I'm hit! Another one! Can't move! I'm . . .

Readers' Theater: On Omaha Beach *(cont.)*

C.J.:   Medic! Medic! The lieutenant's hit.

Sergeant: We've got to go, or we'll all be hit!

Medic: I'll do what I can, boys. Get moving, or you'll all die here with him.

Corporal: You're in charge now, Sergeant! The lieutenant's out of commission.

Sergeant: We go now. Head for the base of the hill. It'll be harder to hit us there. Once we start, keep moving. Don't stop for anything! Every minute on this beach means a higher chance of getting hit. Now go! Move out!

Narrator: The men raced along with hundreds of others toward the base of the hills overlooking the beach, hoping that it would be harder to hit them shooting down from above. They race through a murderous hail of bullets and artillery above them. They run over the fallen bodies of their fellow soldiers knowing that to stop is suicide. This squad of men hurl themselves at the base of the hill and huddle from the storm of fire still coming down at them.

Sergeant: Those guns above us are going to take us out if we don't take them out. Corporal, you and C.J., get those explosives set up. We'll blow up the area beneath those concrete boxes.

Corporal: We're moving. Cover us! Let's go, C.J.

Narrator: C.J. and the corporal climb part of the way up the hill and assemble their explosive devices.

C.J.:   Fire! Fire!

Corporal: C.J.! Answer me! Oh no, C.J.'s dead!

Sergeant: Throw grenades! Aim for the guns. Now!

Narrator: Men from the squad race forward with other members of their platoon. Their grenades land in the pillbox, the concrete bunker where the enemy soldiers were shooting from. The concrete shelter explodes, and the firing inside stops.

Sergeant: That's one down, men. There's plenty more left and right and behind this one. Move out!

Narrator: By the end of the day, Omaha Beach and the other beaches at Normandy were in the hands of the invading army, held by a thin line of courageous men. The cost was terrible, but the liberation of Europe had begun.

Readers' Theater: Crystal Night

There are six speaking parts in this script. Performers can do the rioters' lines as a group.

Narrator: Krystallnacht, or Crystal Night, is the name German Jews gave to the night of November 9, 1938, when mobs of Nazi Party members and their supporters went on a rampage throughout Germany. A Jewish teenager shot a German embassy official in Paris two days earlier resulting in the German's death. This incident was used as a pretext throughout Germany to attack Jews on the streets, to loot and burn their shops, and to burn synagogues. Hannah is a 16-year-old Jewish girl on her way home with her older brother, Daniel, when they are caught in the riot. Jacob and Rosa are their friends.

Hannah: Daniel, we have to get home. The Nazis are everywhere. Our parents are going to be worried. There are mobs on every street.

Daniel: We must be careful. The mobs are looking for anyone. Oh, look at Stein's bakery! The crowd is smashing the windows and looting the place. Those thugs aren't even stealing things to use. They're just throwing the food into the street and destroying the tables and chairs.

Hannah: Why do they hate us so? We never did anything to earn such hatred.

Daniel: They need someone to blame when things go bad. We Jews are good targets. We're easy to recognize, easy to blame, and convenient targets for their loathing. Oh, no! They see us!

Rioters: Jews! Get them! Get those Jews!

Narrator: Hannah and Daniel run for their lives back down the street and run right into a pair of thugs with their hands full of loot. One of the men grabbed Hannah, and Daniel fought with him trying to get his sister free. She ripped loose from his grasp leaving the rioter with a handful of her dress.

Daniel: Run, Hannah! Run!

Hannah: No! Let my brother go!

Rioters: There they are!

Narrator: Hannah kicks one of the thugs in the leg. Daniel pulls loose, grabs his sister's hand and they run down the street, with both groups of rioters in hot pursuit. All of a sudden they turn a corner and see their friends and neighbors, Jacob and Rosa.

Jacob: This way. Through the alley! Run!

Readers' Theater: Crystal Night *(cont.)*

Narrator: The four young Jews race madly down the alley with the mob still in pursuit. All of a sudden, Jacob turns into a narrow space between buildings and leads them to another street. The mob rushes by still looking for victims.

Jacob: The Nazis are wandering the streets grabbing every Jew they can find. They burned my father's printing shop.

Rosa: They looted my father's jewelry store, smashed his cases, and beat him up. Dad told us to go home and take care of our mother.

Jacob: Listen to that howling. Let's see what they're doing.

Narrator: The young Jews quietly look around the corner of the alley they are in to see what's happening on the street to cause such screaming.

Daniel: That's my friend, Erica. I'm going to help her. Jacob, get Hannah home safely!

Narrator: Daniel runs screaming down the alley toward the startled rioters. Jacob, Hannah, and Rosa run after him rather than away. Daniel barrels into the rioters, kicks the one holding Erica and the distraction allows Erica to tear loose from the men holding her. Jacob hits a rioter and Hannah and Rosa grab Erica and flee back down the alley. Jacob races off behind them.

Jacob: There's a hiding place just before the next street! Turn left! Follow the wall of the building. There's the entrance to the cellar. Help me lift the cellar door. Squeeze in! Hurry! I can hear them coming!

Narrator: The young people lift the cellar door and slide down through steps into a cellar below an apartment building.

Erica: (Whispering) Daniel, thank you. Thank you, Hannah! Daniel . . . Daniel?

Jacob: Sssh, Erica! Daniel didn't get away. They held onto him.

Erica: We've got to go help him. Let me out!

Hannah: I'll go with you.

Jacob: No, girls. Daniel knew what he was doing. His fighting and yelling distracted the mob. Maybe he'll get lucky and escape if the mob gets distracted. He wanted you girls safe. We'll stay here for the night and try to make it home in the daylight. Our parents will be frantic but it's our only chance.

Narrator: The Jews called this event Krystallnacht, or Crystal Night, because so much glass was broken in the night of rioting. It was a major step in the Nazi war against the Jews. About 2,000 Jews died as a result of Crystal Night. Jews were no longer just harassed and abused. The Nazis soon began rounding up and deporting Jews to the concentration camps.

Teacher Lesson Plans for Social Studies

Using a Time Line

Objectives: Students will learn to derive information from a time line and add pertinent information to a time line.

Materials: copies of Time Line of 20th Century Wars (pages 64 and 65); reference materials including encyclopedias, textbooks, atlases, almanacs, and Internet sites

Procedure

1. Collect available resources so that students have reference materials in which to find information.

2. Review the concept of a time line, using events from the current school year as an example.

3. Reproduce and distribute the Time Line of 20th Century Wars. Review the various events listed on the time line.

4. Instruct students to place additional dates on the time line as described in the assignment on page 65.

5. Assign or have each student choose one event on the time line to illustrate and label on a separate sheet of paper. Display these illustrations in chronological order on a classroom wall or bulletin board.

Assessment: Assess students' ability to research information. Verify the accuracy of the events and dates that students add to the time line.

Using Maps

Objective: Students will learn to derive and use information from maps.

Materials: copies of Europe Before World War I (page 66); copies of Europe During World War II (page 67); copies of Communism in Europe (page 68); copies of The Middle East (page 69); atlases, almanacs, and other maps for reference and comparison

Procedure

1. Reproduce and distribute the Europe Before World War I map. Review with students the features on a map and how to use a map key. Assign the map activity at the bottom of the page.

2. Reproduce and distribute the Europe During World War II map. Have students color the map as indicated.

3. Reproduce and distribute Communism in Europe map. Have students complete the map activity.

4. Reproduce and distribute The Middle East map. Have students answer the questions and then color the map.

Assessment: Correct the map activity pages together. Check for understanding and review basic concepts as needed.

Teacher Lesson Plans for Social Studies *(cont.)*

Doing Research

Objectives: Students will develop skills in finding, organizing, and presenting research information.

Materials: copies of Researching the Causes and Results of War (page 70); copies of Researching Battles (page 71); copies of Researching 20th Century Leaders (pages 72 and 73); copies of 20th Century Revolutions and Wars (page 74); books, encyclopedias, and Internet sources

Procedure

NOTE: You may choose to let students choose one topic to write about: a war, a battle, or a leader. Another option would be to allow students to give an oral class presentation in lieu of a written report. (In that case, you may want to review with them the Tips for Giving a Speech at the bottom of page 55.)

1. Collect available resources so that students have reference materials in which to find information, or allow students time to go to the school library.

2. Reproduce and distribute copies of Researching the Causes and Results of War. Allow students to choose a 20th century war or conflict to write about. Review the information that should be included. Discuss the need to take notes in an organized manner, the potential sources to use, and the tips at the bottom of the page on how to write a report.

3. Reproduce and distribute Researching Battles. Have students select a battle to write about. Discuss what information to include. Review with students how to find reference materials, take notes, and write the report.

4. Reproduce and distribute both pages of Researching 20th Century Leaders. Review the outline with the class, and let students choose a person on the list (page 73) to research.

5. Reproduce and distribute the 20th Century Revolutions and Wars activity page. Tell students to choose one revolutionary movement to research. Instruct them to complete the Revolution Summary Chart at the bottom of the page.

6. Allow students time to prepare their reports (or oral presentations). If desired, arrange a discussion period where students can share what they learned with the class.

Assessment: Assess students on the basis of their written reports and/or oral presentations.

Time Line of 20th Century Wars

1900 – The Boxer Rebellion in China tries to counteract foreign influences.

1904 – Russia and Japan engage in a two-year war.

1905 – A revolution in Russia reduces the power of the tsar.

1907 – Britain, France, and Russia form an alliance.

1910 – The Mexican Revolution begins.

1914 – The assassination of Archduke Franz Ferdinand of Austria-Hungary leads to World War I.

1917 – Communists seize power in Russia, and Russia withdraws from the war. The United States enters World War I on the Allies' side.

1918 – World War I ends.

1919 – The Treaty of Versailles ends the war, but this peace settlement imposes severe reparations on Germany and forms several new nations. The League of Nations is formed.

1920 – The U S. Congress refuses to ratify the Treaty of Versailles or accept the League of Nations.

1933 – Adolf Hitler becomes dictator of Germany.

1939 – Germany invades Poland, setting off World War II. Britain and France declare war on Germany.

1940 – The Battle of Britain begins. France signs an armistice with Germany.

1941 – Germany invades the Soviet Union. Japan attacks Pearl Harbor, bringing the United States into World War II.

1943 – German forces surrender in Northern Africa. Italy secretly surrenders to the Allies.

1944 – Allied troops land at Normandy, and the reconquest of Europe begins.

1945 – Germany surrenders unconditionally. The first atomic bombs are dropped on two Japanese cities, Hiroshima and Nagasaki, which lead to the surrender of Japan and the end of World War II. The United Nations is established. The North Atlantic Treaty Organization (NATO) is formed to prevent communist expansion.

1948 – The United States sets up the Marshall Plan to help rebuild Europe. The Jewish state of Israel is established.

1949 – Chinese Communist troops conquer China.

1950 – Communist North Korean troops invade South Korea, starting the Korean War. South Korean and American troops are pushed south to the Pusan Perimeter. American troops land at Inchon and move north. Chinese troops enter the Korean War.

1953 – An armistice ends fighting in Korea.

1955 – Communist nations sign the Warsaw Pact to counteract NATO.

1957 – Communist Viet Cong rebel against the Diem government in South Vietnam.

Time Line of 20th Century Wars *(cont.)*

1959 – Fidel Castro leads communists to power in a Cuban revolution.

1961 – Communists erect the Berlin Wall, dividing East and West Germany.

1962 – The Cuban Missile Crisis brings the world to the brink of nuclear war.

1963 – South Vietnamese generals overthrow the Diem government.

– President John F. Kennedy is assassinated.

1964 – The U.S. Congress passes the Gulf of Tonkin Resolution, authorizing the president to use force in Vietnam.

1965 – President Johnson sends the first U.S. ground troops to Da Nang, South Vietnam.

1966 – Chinese dictator Mao Zedong begins a massive Cultural Revolution against traditional beliefs and behaviors.

1967 – Israel wins the Six Day War against Arab nations.

1968 – North Vietnam and their Viet Cong allies launch the Tet Offensive against South Vietnam cities.

– Soviet troops invade Czechoslovakia to put down an uprising.

1969 – The U.S. begins gradual withdrawal of troops from Vietnam.

1973 – The U.S. and North Vietnam sign a cease-fire agreement, and the last U.S. troops leave Vietnam.

1975 – South Vietnam surrenders to North Vietnam.

1978 – Vietnam invades Cambodia.

1979 – Russia invades Afghanistan.

1980 – The Polish trade union Solidarity is formed to combat Russian forces in Poland.

– An eight-year war begins between Iran and Iraq.

1989 – Democratic reformers establish non-Communist governments in former Soviet nations.

1990 – East and West Germany are reunited.

1991 – The U.S. wins the Gulf War, forcing Iraqi troops to withdraw from Kuwait which they had invaded.

– A civil war begins in Yugoslavia, and the country falls into chaos.

2003 – The United States attacks Iraq and removes Saddam Hussein from power.

Assignment

Find at least 10 dates in world history to add to the above time line. These dates could include revolutions, wars, inventions, elections, assassinations, scientific achievements, disasters, cultural fads, or sporting events. Then choose one of these events to illustrate, color, and label on a separate sheet of paper. Be sure to include the date.

Europe Before World War I

Directions: Use the map to name the Allied powers, Central powers, and neutral countries.

Name the Allied powers. (Five are not shown on the map.)

_____

_____

_____

_____

Name the Central powers.

_____

_____

Name the Neutral countries.

_____

_____

_____

Europe During World War II

Directions: Color the map of Europe as indicated below.

1. Use red for the Axis nations: Germany, Italy, Finland, Hungary, Bulgaria, and Romania.

2. Use green for the Allied nations that were overrun by Germany: Poland, France, Norway, Luxembourg, Yugoslavia, Czechoslovakia, parts of the Soviet Union, Albania, Austria, Greece, and Denmark. Also include the Baltic nations of Latvia, Lithuania, and Estonia.

3. Use yellow for the neutral nations: Spain, Portugal, Switzerland, Sweden, and Ireland.

4. Use purple for the Allies that were not overrun by Germany: Great Britain and Turkey.

5. Use blue for the bodies of water: Atlantic Ocean, Baltic Sea, Black Sea, Mediterranean Sea, and Arctic Ocean.

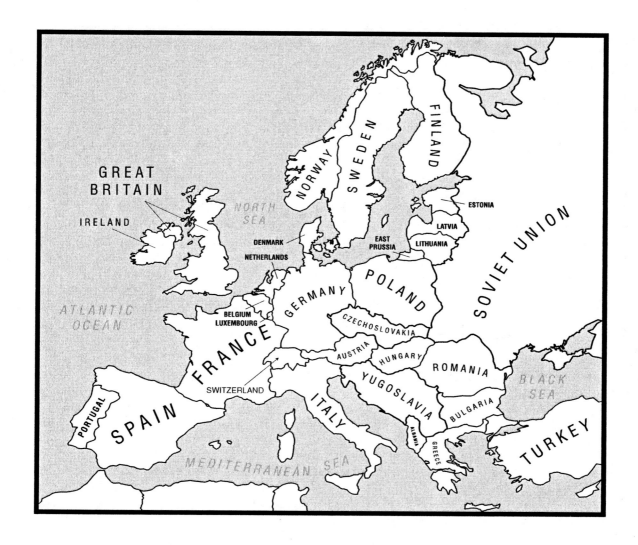

Communism in Europe

Directions: Use the map below to list the communist countries.

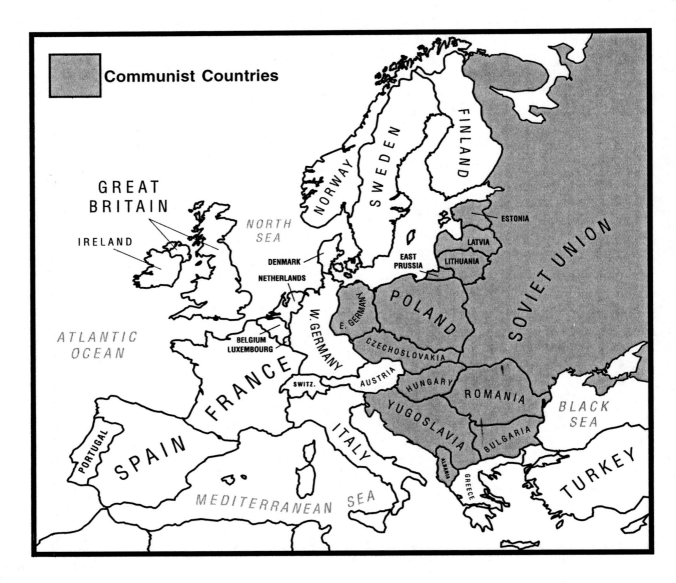

List European countries controlled or influenced by the Soviet Union after World War II.

1. _____   5. _____

2. _____   6. _____

3. _____   7. _____

4. _____   8. _____

The Middle East

Directions: Use the map below to answer the following questions.

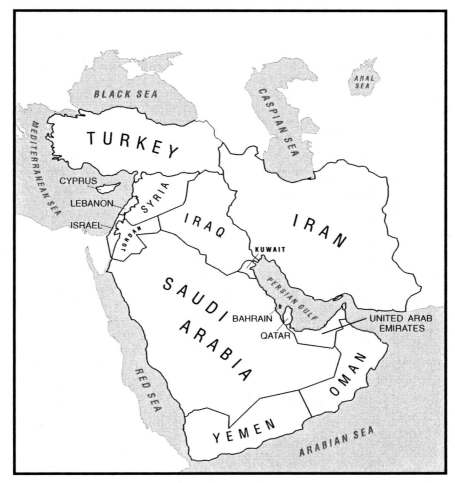

1. What is the largest Middle Eastern country?_____

2. What are Israel's three Middle Eastern neighbors?_____

3. What six countries surround the Persian Gulf?_____

_____

4. What four Middle Eastern countries border the Mediterranean Sea? _____

5. What two Middle Eastern countries face the Arabian Sea? _____

6. What sea is north of Turkey? _____

7. What sea is north of Iran? _____

Researching the Causes and Results of War

20th Century Wars and Conflicts

There were many wars and conflicts in the 20th century. Some of them involved all the major countries in the world with fighting scattered around the globe. Others were smaller and were centered in one country between rival nations. The century's main military clashes are listed below.

- Arab-Israeli conflicts
- Balkan Wars
- Iraq-Iran War
- Korean War
- Persian Gulf War
- Russo-Japanese War
- Vietnam War
- World War I
- World War II

Assignment

Choose a specific war or conflict from the above list. Research the causes and results of that conflict. Use the following questions and the tips at the bottom of the page to help write your report.

1. Who were the first nations to get involved in the conflict?
2. What single event or action started the war?
3. Who were the leaders and how did their attitudes lead to war?
4. What religious, racial, or ethnic prejudices helped push toward war rather than a peaceful resolution?
5. How did misunderstanding and distrust lead to war?
6. Which country, in your opinion, was more anxious for war? Give your reasons.
7. Which country was more prepared for war?
8. Which country or countries won the war?
9. What was the cost of the war in terms of lives lost?
10. Which countries were largely destroyed by the conflict?
11. Which countries, if any, achieved their independence from other countries because of the war?
12. Which nations became more powerful because of the defeat of another country?
13. What were the unexpected results of the war?

Writing a Report

When writing a report, it is important to do the following:

- Use as many sources as possible, including textbooks, encyclopedias, Internet web sites, and books.
- Take notes carefully. Get all of the facts, but it is not necessary to use complete sentences in notes. Be sure to write down where you found the information, however, so you can refer back to it if needed or include the reference on the bibliography or works-cited page.
- Organize the notes by time and place, and use them to help you write the report.
- Use your own words. Do **not** copy sentences word-for-word from your sources. This is called *plagiarism,* which means "stealing and passing off someone else's work as your own without giving credit to that person."
- Check spelling, especially of unfamiliar names and places.
- Carefully check your report for correct grammar, punctuation, margins, and other writing conventions.
- Neatly write or type the final copy of the report in paragraph format.

Researching Battles

Assignment

Choose a battle from the list at the bottom of the page that took place in a war fought in the 20th century. Research that battle, and write a report about it. Take notes, and include the following information about the battle. Use the Writing a Report tips at the bottom of page 70 to help you.

- Date of the battle
- Place of the battle (country, city, town, river, etc.)
- Number of days the battle lasted
- Military commanders in charge of each side
- Important leaders involved in the actual battle
- Numbers of fighting men on each side
- Problems faced by each army or navy
- Weapons used by each side
- Special acts of bravery during the battle (leading a charge, fighting against a vastly superior number, etc.)
- How the battle came to be (what each army was trying to do)
- Effects of the weather and geography on the battle
- Results of the battle (who won, effect on the war's outcome)

Extension

Draw a map of the battle you researched. Include all the information you can about the battle. Show where each army began the battle, and use arrows on the map to show the movement of the military.

20th Century Battles

World War I

Battle of Jutland
Battle of Vimy Ridge
Belleau Wood
Chateau-Thierry
Marne
Meuse-Argonne Offensive
Siegfried Line
Somme
The Dardanelles
Verdun
Ypres

World War II

Anzio
Bataan
Battle of Britain
Battle of the Atlantic

Cassino
Coral Sea
El Alamein
German Invasion of Poland
German Invasion of Russia
Guadalcanal
Invasion of Normandy
Invasion of Sicily
Invasion of the Low Countries
Iwo Jima
Kasserine Pass
Leyte Gulf
Midway
Pearl Harbor
Salerno
Stalingrad

Korean War

Battle for the Hills
Changjin Reservoir
Inchon Landing
Pusan Perimeter

Vietnam War

Da Nang
Dien Bien Phu
Ke Sanh
Hue
Invasion of Cambodia
Invasion of Laos
Mekong Delta
Pleiku
Saigon
Tet Offensive

Researching 20th Century Leaders

Assignment

Choose a 20th century leader from the list on page 73. Use the outline below to help you research important information about that leader

---

Biographical Outline

I. Youth

   A. Birth place and date

   B. Home life and experiences

      1. Brothers and sisters

      2. Places lived

      3. Circumstances (rich, poor, etc.)

   C. Schooling

   D. Childhood ambitions/heroes

   E. Interesting childhood facts and stories

II. Leadership

   A. Lifestyle and personal habits

      1. Values and beliefs

      2. Personal qualities (cruel, kind, honest, etc.)

   B. War experiences

      1. Country or people fought for

      2. Battles fought in (give details)

      3. Dangers faced (give details)

      4. Leadership experiences

   C. Reasons for fame

      1. Contributions to war effort

      2. Accomplishments

      3. Failures and struggles

      4. Greatest challenges faced

   D. Contemporaries

      1. Co-workers/colleagues

      2. Presidents and public leaders

III. Death

   A. Date and place

   B. Age

   C. Cause

Researching 20th Century Leaders *(cont.)*

Military Leaders

Bernard Montgomery—senior British general in WWII

Douglas MacArthur—U.S. general and hero in WWII

Dwight D. Eisenhower— U.S. commander in Europe

Erwin Rommel—brilliant German general

Hideki Tojo—Japan's leader during WWII

George C. Marshall—U.S. planner during WWII

George Patton—superior U.S. tank strategist

Georgi Zhukov—great Russian general during WWII

Isoroku Yamamoto—Japanese commander at Pearl Harbor

John "Blackjack" Pershing—led U.S. troops in WWI

Joseph Stilwell— U.S. general in Asia during WWII

Norman Schwarzkopf—commander in the Persian Gulf

Omar Bradley—U.S. general in WWII

Political Leaders

Adolf Hitler—German dictator during WWII

Archduke Franz Ferdinand—His assassination started WWI

Benito Mussolini—Italy's fascist dictator

Chiang Kai-shek—moderate Chinese leader during WWII

Francisco Franco—Nazi leader in Spain

Franklin D. Roosevelt—U.S. president during WWII

Golda Meir—Israeli prime minister

Harry Truman—U.S. president at the end of WWII

Ho Chi Minh—North Vietnam's revolutionary leader

John F. Kennedy—U.S. president who clashed with Russia

Joseph Stalin—Russian leader during WWII

Kaiser Wilhelm II—Germany's emperor during WWI

Kim Il Sung—North Korean dictator for over 40 years

Lyndon B. Johnson—president during the Vietnam conflict

Mao Zedong—communist dictator in China

Mohandas Gandhi—leader in gaining India's independence

Ngo Dinh Diem—leader of South Vietnam

Nikita Khrushchev—Russian leader who put missiles in Cuba

Richard Nixon—president during Vietnam War

Saddam Hussein—Iraqi dictator who clashed with U.S.

Vladimir Lenin—Russia's revolutionary leader

Winston Churchill—British prime minister during WWII

Woodrow Wilson—U.S. president during WWI

Other Leaders

Ayatollah Khomeini—Iranian religious revolutionary

Bill Mauldin—popular WWII cartoonist

Ernie Pyle—U.S. journalist and war correspondent

20th Century Revolutions and Wars

The 20th century witnessed efforts by millions of people to attain freedom. Some people wanted to change the type of government and remove a ruler or a dictator. Others wanted to be free from control or mistreatment by other nations, religious groups, or ethnic groups.

Assignment

Choose one revolution or liberation movement from the list below. Complete the following chart using as many sources as possible, including textbooks, encyclopedias, Internet web sites, and other sources. Share what you learn with a small group or the entire class.

Political Revolutions (replacing a government)

- Chinese Revolution
- Mexican Revolution
- Russian Revolution
- Spanish Civil War
- Turkish Revolution

Ethnic Revolutions (freedom from control by other countries)

- Afghanistan Rebellion against Soviet Union
- Armenian Independence Movement
- Balkan National Revolution
- Egyptian and other Arab national revolts against colonialism
- Indian Independence Movement
- Ireland Freedom Movement
- Kenyan and other African revolts against colonial rule
- Korean Revolution
- Kurdish Independence Movement
- Vietnamese Revolution

Revolution Summary Chart

Name of revolution: _____

Time period: _____

People seeking liberation: _____

Where the revolution took place: _____

Type of government or group controlling those seeking freedom: _____

_____

Reasons people were being oppressed (race, religion, dictatorship): _____

_____

Who or what influenced the revolutionary movement: _____

_____

Results of the movement (new nation or government, fairer laws): _____

_____

_____

Teacher Lesson Plans for Science, Math, Music, and Art

Inventions and Science Projects

Objectives: Students will learn about 20th century inventions and make or conduct simple science projects related to war.

Materials: copies of 20th Century Inventions (page 77); copies of Model Helicopters (page 78); copies of Paper Airplanes (pages 79 and 80); copies of Anchors Aweigh (page 81); copies of Parachute Drop (page 82); copies of Weather and Temperature (page 83); encyclopedias or other reference materials; science materials listed on each page, including protective eyewear, small paper clips, large paper clips, fishing line, straws, scissors, pencils, 8½" by 11" (22 cm x 28 cm) paper, clear tape, thermometers, rulers, aluminum foil, pennies or crayons, plastic tubs, masking tape, hole punch

Procedure

NOTE: Collect the materials listed on each page before assigning the project.

1. Reproduce and distribute the 20th Century Inventions activity sheet. Review the assignment and provide reference materials for students to use. Have students complete the assignment independently or with a partner.

2. Reproduce and distribute the Model Helicopters activity sheet. Review the directions for making the first model spinner. Allow students to practice using it. Have them make the remaining two models and test them also. Discuss their results.

3. Reproduce and distribute the Paper Airplanes activity sheets. Review the directions for making the paper airplane. Let students practice flying their planes. Then have students make the modifications suggested on page 80. Review the results after a period of trial and experimentation. If desired, have a contest to see whose plane flies the farthest.

4. Reproduce and distribute the Anchors Aweigh activity sheet. Review the directions for making the first boat. Encourage students to do several trials to see how much weight it will hold. Then have students make the second model and test it. Finally, have students make their own designs and test them. Discuss the results and what design worked best.

5. Reproduce and distribute the Parachute Drop activity sheet. Review the directions for making the model parachute. Allow students to test the model parachute several times. Then have students make their own designs and test them. Discuss their results.

6. Reproduce and distribute the Weather and Temperature activity sheet. Review the directions for recording temperature and climate at selected times. Review the procedures for finding the measures of central tendency. Let students share their findings.

Assessment: Correct the Inventions activity sheet together. Evaluate students' ability to follow directions in making the science projects. Evaluate students' Weather and Temperature activity sheet together.

Teacher Lesson Plans for Science, Math, Music, and Art *(cont.)*

Math Statistics

Objective: Students will apply their math skills to organizing and working with statistics.
Materials: copies of World War I Statistics (page 84); copies of World War II Statistics (page 85); copies of U.S. War Statistics (page 86); copies of Baseball in Wartime (page 87); calculators
Procedure
1. Reproduce and distribute the World War I Statistics activity sheet. Review the assignment and the math processes involved, especially how to calculate percentages. Have students complete the activity sheet independently.
2. Reproduce and distribute the World War II Statistics activity sheet. Review the assignment and the math processes involved. Have students complete the activity sheet independently.
3. Reproduce and distribute the U.S. War Statistics activity sheet. Review the assignment and the math processes involved. Have students complete the activity sheet independently. As an extension, have students make a bar graph.
4. Reproduce and distribute the Baseball in Wartime activity sheet. As a class, read about and discuss the women's baseball league. Have students complete the assignment independently or with a partner to find out what percentage of the class plays baseball. As an extension, have students find out which states the women's baseball teams were from.

Assessment: Correct the activity sheets together. Review math concepts as needed.

Songs

Objective: Students will learn about wartime songs and the role music plays in an era.
Materials: copies of Wartime Songs (page 88); a recording of the song "Over There" and other wartime songs (if possible); copies of the lyrics to popular wartime songs
Procedure
1. Reproduce and distribute the Wartime Songs activity sheet. If possible, play a recording of the song "Over There." Discuss why the song was written and the effect that a song's words and tune can have on listeners.
2. Have students complete the assignment independently. Provide songbooks or reference materials with the lyrics to wartime songs, or instruct students to search the Internet.
3. As an extension, have students watch a movie (in class or at home) about a 20th century war and then write a review of it.

Assessment: Evaluate students' ability to find information and make inferences about it.

Posters

Objective: Students will design and create a visual presentation.
Materials: copies of Rationing (page 89); poster board; markers
Procedure
1. Reproduce and distribute the Rationing activity sheet. Read the page together.
2. Have students complete the assignment, making posters independently or with a partner. Allow them to share their finished work, and then display them around the room.
3. As an extension, have students make a patriotic poster or a military recruitment poster.

Assessment: Evaluate students' posters for content and presentation of the topic.

20th Century Inventions

The 20th century witnessed a flood of inventions designed to make life easier for workers. Many of these inventions were also used toward war efforts.

Assignment

Match the inventions in the column on the right with the inventor, date, and description listed in the left-hand column. Use an encyclopedia or the Internet to help you if needed.

Inventors

_____ 1. Ernst Ruska—1932, a machine to see the smallest things

_____ 2. Clarence Birdseye and Charles Seabrook—1925, food preservation

_____ 3. Godfrey Hounsfield and Allan Cormack—1972, more detail about the human body

_____ 4. Jonas Salk—1954, a cure for a crippling disease

_____ 5. Wallace Carothers—1935, used in parachutes, jackets, and women's stockings

_____ 6. Alexander Fleming—1928, kills infections

_____ 7. Frank Whittle—1930, a revolutionary improvement in the airplane

_____ 8. Igor Sikorsky—1939, aircraft that takes off and lands vertically

_____ 9. Orville and Wilbur Wright—1903, getting off the ground

_____ 10. John Eckert, John Manchly, and John Atanasoff—1946, it counts faster than a person

_____ 11. Robert Watson-Watt—1935, it can track an airplane

_____ 12. Philo Farnsworth—1928, it brings the world and entertainment to people's homes

Inventions

a. airplane

b. CAT scan

c. electronic digital computer

d. electronic microscope

e. frozen food

f. helicopter

g. jet engine

h. nylon

i. penicillin

j. polio vaccine

k. radar

l. television

Extension

Choose one of the following activities.

- Make a timeline showing each of the above inventions. Include pictures of the inventions.

- Create a PowerPoint presentation about some of the major 20th century inventions.

Model Helicopters

Helicopters are vertical-lift aircrafts. They are lifted and flown by rotating blades, which are airfoils. Make the models below. Notice how much weight they can lift.

Making a Simulated Helicopter

Materials: protective eyewear, fishing line 18 inches (46 cm) long, 1 small paper clip, several large paper clips, 1 straw, scissors, tape

Procedure

1. Tie one end of the fishing line to the small paper clip.

2. Cut the straw in half.

3. Put the fishing line through the half-straw.

4. Tape the 4 large paper clips into a bundle.

5. Tie the other end of the fishing line to the bundle of large paper clips.

Using the Helicopter

SAFETY NOTE: Students must wear protective eyewear and stay at least three feet away from others when using this model.

1. Put the bundle of large paper clips in one hand.

2. Hold the straw in the middle with three fingers, and gently spin the small paper clip in a circular motion until it is whirling.

3. The small whirling paper clip should lift the bundle of large paper clips and pull them against the bottom of the straw.

Adjusting the Helicopter

1. Add another large paper clip to the bundle. Does the small, rotating paper clip lift the extra weight?

2. Keep adding paper clips and testing your model. How many large paper clips can the model lift?

3. Remove the extra paper clips, and tape the 4 large paper clips into a bundle again.

4. Bend the small paper clip into an "S" shape.

5. Test the model. Does it work better or worse?

6. Put tape around each loop in the "S." Does it work better or worse?

7. Bend the loops in different directions. What is the result? Which model worked best?

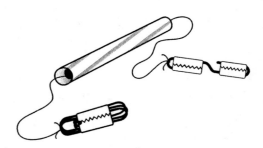

Paper Airplanes

Airplanes were first used by the military in World War I. Today military aircraft have become very advanced and are used by armies, air forces, and navies around the world. Jet fighters attack other aircraft, bombers drop bombs or fire missiles, transport aircraft carry troops and vehicles, and reconnaissance aircraft gather information and spy on the enemy. Follow the directions below for making a paper airplane.

Making the Airplane

Materials: 8½" x 11" (22 cm x 28 cm) sheet of paper, 1 or 2 small paper clips, clear tape, ruler, pencil

1. Measure and draw a line 2" (5 cm) up from the bottom of the paper.

2. Fold the top down to the line you drew. Crease the fold.

3. Measure 1½" (4 cm) down from the top fold. Draw a line. Neatly fold the paper along the line.

4. Fold in half down the center of the paper so that each side is symmetrical.

5. Measure 1" (2.54 cm) in from the center fold, and draw a line. Fold the wing down along the line.

6. Turn the paper over and do the same on the other side.

7. Fold each corner down along the 1" (2.54 cm) lines. Tape the wings in place.

8. Measure and draw a line ½" (1.3 cm) from the edge of each wing. Fold down along each line to make the rudders.

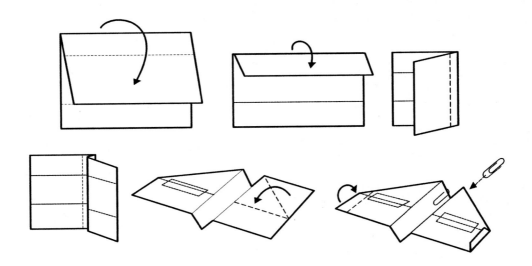

Flying the Airplane

1. The weight of a paper plane should be in the nose. Place a small paper clip on each side of the nose as shown.

2. Hold the plane along the fuselage between your thumb and middle finger. Place your index finger against the rear of the plane. Release the plane as you snap your wrist forward.

Paper Airplanes *(cont.)*

The Four Forces of Flight

There are four forces which affect flight:

1. **Lift**—the force that causes the wing to rise into the air

2. **Thrust**—the force that moves a plane forward

3. **Gravity**—the downward pull on the airplane

4. **Drag**—the air resistance or friction slowing down a plane moving through the air

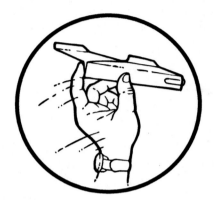

Working With the Forces of Flight

1. Examine the paper airplane you made using the directions on page 79. Lift increases when the underside of the wings is flat and the upper side is curved. Is your plane designed this way?

2. What provides the thrust for your plane? Try different techniques for holding and launching your plane. What works best for you?

3. Try folding the rudders the opposite way. How does this affect the flight characteristics of your plane? Fold one rudder up and one rudder down. How does this affect the plane's flight?

4. Use only one paper clip on the nose of the plane to hold the fuselage tight. Fly the plane and observe the results.

5. Change the shape of the wings by changing the corner folds. How does this affect the airplane's flight?

Design Your Own Plane

Using the same materials listed on page 79, design a plane of your own. Remember the four principles of flight. Also keep the following things in mind when making your plane.

- Much of the weight of a paper plane should be in the nose.

- The underside should be flat and smooth.

- The upper side should at least be curved slightly.

- Throwing the plane too hard can result in too much drag.

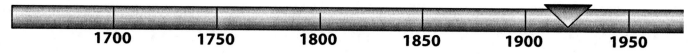
Anchors Aweigh

Boats and ships of every type were improved in the 20th century, partly as a result of war. Nations wanted bigger ships to carry more soldiers and military supplies across the oceans. They also wanted faster and more powerful warships.

Follow the directions below to make three different boats and find out how shape and design affect the amount of weight a boat can carry. Test each design and make adjustments until you find the best one.

Materials: 3 pieces of aluminum foil 4" x 12" inches long (10 cm x 30 cm), plastic tub or other container with 2 to 3 inches (5 cm to 8 cm) of water, scissors, and pennies, large paper clips, or crayons for weights

Model 1

1. Fold each side of one of the aluminum foil pieces up 1" (2.54 cm) from the edge.

2. Make a 1" (2.54 cm) diagonal cut at each of the four corners.

3. Overlap the foil pieces at each corner.

4. Put your model boat in the water, and make sure it floats.

5. Add weight—pennies, paper clips, or crayons—one at a time to the foil boat, and see how many you can put in it before the boat sinks.

Model 2

1. Take the second piece of aluminum foil and fold it into a canoe shape.

2. Put your model in the water, and keep adding weight to see how much it can carry. Does it hold more weight that the first boat?

Model 3

1. Use the third piece of aluminum foil to make a model boat of your own design.

2. Put the boat in the water. How well does it float?

3. Add weight, one at a time. Does it hold more weight than the Model 1 or 2 boat? Which design worked the best? Why do you think that is?

Parachute Drop

Parachutes were essential to pilots who might be shot down by enemy fire. Make a working model by following these directions.

Making the Chute

Materials: 8½" by 11" (22 cm x 28 cm) sheet of paper, scissors, 4 pieces of fishing line that are each 1' (30 cm) long, ruler, 4 large paper clips, masking tape, hole punch

Procedure

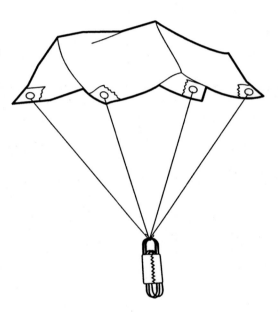

1. Fold the 8½" by 11" paper in half and then in half again.

2. Use the hole punch (or scissors) to make a hole about ½" (1.3 cm) from the edge in each corner.

3. Reverse one of the four fold lines so that all four folds face the same way.

4. Tie one end of a piece of fishing line to one of the large paper clips, and then tie the other end to one corner of the paper. Use masking tape to hold it securely.

5. Follow the same procedure in step 4 for the other three pieces of fishing line.

6. Take the four paper clips attached to the paper and tape them so that the parachute is balanced. Note that the paper clips may need to be adjusted slightly if they are at different lengths.

Testing the Chute

1. Throw the parachute into the air. Does it land evenly? Do several trials, making adjustments as needed.

2. Make a parachute using some of the following materials: newspapers, plastic trash bags, paper towels, handkerchiefs, heavier weights such as small batteries or film canisters. Test it. How does it compare to the parachute made out of paper?

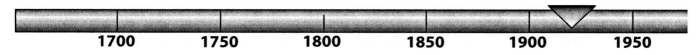

Weather and Temperature

Many battles from the D-Day invasion of Normandy to the Battle of Stalingrad to the retreat at the "Frozen Chosun" in Korea were influenced by weather conditions and the temperature.

Assignment

Use a thermometer to record the temperature at your school or home three times a day for five days. Record the basic weather conditions (for example: drizzle, heavy rain, sunshine, snow, or cloudy). Then answer the questions below the chart.

	Day 1	**Day 2**	**Day 3**	**Day 4**	**Day 5**
Time 1					
Temperature					
Conditions					
Time 2					
Temperature					
Conditions					
Time 3					
Temperature					
Conditions					

1. Highest recorded temperature: _____

2. Lowest recorded temperature: _____

3. Least to greatest (list all of the temperatures in order from least to greatest, including any duplicate temperatures):_____

   _____

4. Range (subtract the lowest from highest): _____

5. Mode (most frequently repeated temperature, if any): _____

6. Median (the middle number of the 15 temperatures): _____

7. Mean (add all 15 temperatures together and divide by 15): _____

Extension

The weather often affects the things you do. Answer the questions below on a separate sheet of paper.

1. What are some activities you can do when the weather is: Rainy? Snowy? Sunny? Windy? Cloudy?

2. What are some activities you cannot do when the weather is: Rainy? Snowy? Sunny? Windy? Cloudy?

3. What is your favorite type of weather and temperature? Why?

World War I Statistics

Directions: Use the statistics to solve the math word problems below. Show your work on the back of this page.

1. The Allied Powers in World War I mobilized 42,000,000 men to fight, and 12,000,000 of these soldiers were from Russia. What percentage of the Allied soldiers were Russian?

   _____

2. The British Empire mobilized 9,000,000 soldiers of the 42,000,000 Allied troops. What percentage of the soldiers were British?

   _____

3. Russia suffered 1,700,000 deaths, 4,950,000 wounded, and 2,500,000 prisoners and missing. What were Russia's total casualties?

   _____

4. Germany suffered 1,773,700 dead, 4,216,058 wounded, and 1,152,800 prisoners and missing. What were Germany's total casualties?

   _____

5. Germany mobilized 11,000,000 troops. Austria-Hungary had 7,800,000 soldiers. Turkey called up 2,850,000 troops, and Bulgaria mobilized 1,200,000 troops. What was the total number of Central powers troops?

   _____

6. Austria-Hungary mobilized 7,800,000 troops. They suffered 7,020,000 casualties. What was Austria-Hungary's percentage of casualties?

   _____

7. The Allied powers had 5,152,115 troops killed. The Central powers had 8,538,315 troops killed. How many more soldiers died fighting for the Central powers than the Allies?

   _____

8. Of its 8,410,000 troops, France suffered 6,160,800 casualties. What percentage of casualties did France have?

   _____

9. The United States mobilized 4,355,000 troops and suffered a casualty rate of 8.2%. How many casualties did the United States have?

   _____

10. Montenegro mobilized 50,000 soldiers and suffered a 40% casualty rate. How many casualties did they suffer?

    _____

World War II Statistics

Directions: Use the statistics to solve the math word problems below. Show your work on the back of this page.

1. The United States suffered 407,000 military deaths in World War II, and Great Britain had 388,000. How many more Americans died than British?

   _____

2. The Soviet Union losses included 13,600,000 military deaths and 7,700,000 civilian deaths. How many casualties did they have altogether?

   _____

3. Of the 6 million civilian deaths in Poland, 2.9 million were Jews. How many of the civilian deaths were not Jews?

   _____

4. World War II cost the Soviet Union 21,300,000 lives. It cost the United States 407,000 lives. How many more Soviets were killed than Americans?

   _____

5. Germany's losses totaled 3,250,000 soldiers and 3,810,000 civilian lives. How many losses did Germany have altogether?

   _____

6. China suffered 1,324,000 military deaths and 10,000,000 civilian deaths. How many more civilians were killed than soldiers?

   _____

7. Russia fatalities were 21,300,000 lives. Germany lost 7,060,000 lives. What was the percentage of German losses compared to Russia's?

   _____

8. Poland lost 6,850,000 lives, and 6,000,000 of those were civilians. What percentage of Poland's losses were civilians?

   _____

9. Total World War II deaths were estimated at 52 million lives. Japan's losses numbered about 2 million. What percentage of the total deaths were Japanese?

   _____

10. What percentage of the 52 million deaths in World War II did Germany suffer if it had about 7 million deaths?

   _____

U.S. War Statistics

Directions: Use the statistics to solve the math word problems below. Show your work on the bottom and back of this page.

1. The United States had 16,353,659 people in the military during World War II. Casualties (wounded and dead) were 1,079,162. How many Americans were not wounded or killed?

    _____

2. The United States had a population of 132 million at the beginning of World War II, and 16.4 million Americans served in the military. What percentage of the U.S. population served in the military?

    _____

3. Out of a population of about 100 million people, the U.S. had 4.7 million soldiers in military service in World War I. What percentage of Americans were in the military?

    _____

4. Some 8,752,000 soldiers served in the Vietnam War. In the Korean War, the number of soldiers was 5,764,143. How many more soldiers served in Vietnam than in Korea?

    _____

5. Out of the 467,939 American soldiers who served in the Persian Gulf War, American casualties totaled 766. What percentage of those serving were casualties?

    _____

6. In the Vietnam War, there were about 211,000 American casualties of which about 58,000 died. What percentage of the casualties were killed?

    _____

7. Some 794,000 U.S. Marines served in Vietnam. In the Korean War, approximately 424,000 Marines served. How many more Marines served in Vietnam than in Korea?

    _____

8. Of the 8,750,000 Americans in military service during the Vietnam War, about 2,600,000 soldiers actually served in Vietnam during the conflict. What percentage of U.S. soldiers served in Vietnam?

    _____

9. In Vietnam, about 38,000 Army servicemen were killed and about 15,000 Marines were killed. What was the percentage of Marines killed compared to Army personnel?

    _____

10. The U.S. had 4.7 million soldiers in World War I and 16.4 million in World War II. How many more served in World War II than World War I?

    _____

Extension

On a separate sheet of paper, make a bar graph that shows the number of Americans who served in World War I, World War II, the Korean War, and the Vietnam War.

Baseball in Wartime

In the first 60 years of the 20th century, baseball was the dominant sport in American culture. When World War II began, some people wanted to suspend baseball for the duration of the war. President Roosevelt and other leaders felt the games should continue because they were good for the national morale. However, most of the ballplayers joined the military, so in 1943 Philip K. Wrigley, the millionaire chewing-gum mogul and owner of the Chicago Cubs, organized a league which eventually became the All-American Girls Professional Baseball League. The league started with four teams located in small mid-western cities: the Rockford Peaches (Illinois), the South Bend Blue Sox (Indiana), the Racine Belles (Wisconsin), and the Kenosha Comets (Wisconsin). They played a 108-game schedule, and by 1948 the league had 10 teams and drew more than a million paying fans. By its conclusion in 1954, nearly 600 women had played in the league, and there had been teams in 14 cities.

Some of the main differences with the women's game were the size of the baseball diamond, the size of the ball, and the pitching styles. The female ballplayers earned between $55 and $85 a week. They were required to wear short skirts while playing and had to wear lipstick at all times. They were not allowed to wear pants at any time, and it was preferred that they have long hair. The 1992 movie *A League of Their Own* (rated PG) was a fictional story that told about the founding of this league. In 1988 the National Baseball Hall of Fame in Cooperstown, New York, added a special exhibit to honor the women's league and its players.

Over the past 20 years, many girls have played on coed Little League teams, and some women have even played on college baseball teams with men. Today nearly three million girls and 300,000 women play amateur baseball.

Assignment

Take a poll to find out how many of your classmates play baseball.

1. How many students are in your class? _____ girls _____ boys _____ total
2. How many play baseball? _____ girls _____ boys _____ total
3. What percentage of the class plays baseball? _____ girls _____ boys _____ total

Extension

Find out what states the women's baseball teams were from.

All-American Girls Professional Baseball League

Below are the names of the teams in the women's league. The years each team existed are listed in parentheses.

- Battle Creek Belles (1951–1952)
- Chicago Colleens (1948)
- Fort Wayne Daisies (1945–1954)
- Grand Rapids Chicks (1945–1954)
- Kalamazoo Lassies (1950–1954)
- Kenosha Comets (1943–1951)
- Milwaukee Chicks (1944)
- Minneapolis Millerettes (1944)
- Muskegon Belles (1953)
- Muskegon Lassies (1946–1949)
- Peoria Redwings (1946–1951)
- Racine Belles (1943–1950)
- Rockford Peaches (1943–1954)
- South Bend Blue Sox (1943–1954)
- Springfield Sallies (1948)

Wartime Songs

Music plays a large part in every era. It reflects what is happening during that time period, and tells how people are feeling. During World War I and World War II, American soldiers went overseas with enthusiasm and pride. The songs written about war encouraged fathers, sons, and husbands who had left home to fight in the war. These songs were heard throughout homes in America and also on the battlefields. Songs written in the latter part of the 20th century sometimes reflected a different sentiment about war. In particular, they questioned America's military involvement overseas.

Read the words to the chorus of the famous World War I song "Over There" by George M. Cohan. If possible, listen to a recording of the song. Why do you think it was a popular song? How does it make you feel?

"Over There"

Over there, over there
Send the word, send the word, over there
That the Yanks are coming, the Yanks are coming,
The drums rum tumming everywhere.

So prepare, say a prayer
Send the word, send the word to beware
We'll be over, we're coming over.
And we won't be back till it's over over there!

Assignment

Use the Internet or other sources to find the words to another song that told about being in combat or on the home front during a 20th century conflict. Share the lyrics with the class. If possible, play a recording of the song. Write a review of the song, highlighting how it affected people and their attitudes and feelings about the war.

Extension

Watch a movie about a war in the 20th century, and then write a review of it. What conflict did it tell about? What happened in the movie? Was it a true story? Was it realistic? What did you learn about the war? Would you recommend the movie to others?

Popular Wartime-Era Songs

World War I
"I Didn't Raise My Boy to Be a Soldier"
"Oh, How I Hate to Get Up in the Morning!"
"You're in the Army Now!"

World War II
"Boogie Woogie Bugle Boy"
"Praise the Lord and Pass the Ammunition"
"The White Cliffs of Dover"
"When the Lights Go on Again"

Vietnam War
"Ballad of the Green Berets"
"Born in the U.S.A."
"The Great Mandala (The Wheel Of Life)"
"The I Feel Like I'm Fixin' to Die Rag"
"The Times They Are A-Changin"
"Universal Soldier"
"War"
"Where Have All the Flowers Gone?"

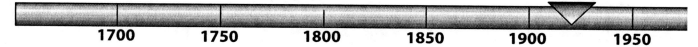
Rationing

A popular motto during World War II was "Use it up, wear it out, make it do, or do without." It reminded Americans on the home front to do their part for the war effort. Soldiers' needs came before those people at home. To ensure that U.S. soldiers would not lack essential supplies, a system of *rationing* was instituted. The government set limits on gasoline, rubber, certain foods, and other vital supplies.

Food rationing started gradually with items like sugar and coffee but soon became a fairly complicated system of points and coupons. The Office of Price Controls (OPC) was created to set limits on items. It began the rationing of a wide variety of items including food, gasoline, and even shoes.

Each American was given a set number of ration coupons per month. Coupons worth blue points were used to purchase processed foods such as canned vegetables, jellies, and bottled tomato juice. Red point coupons were needed to buy meat, butter, cheese, and other fats. When a particular item was purchased, the correct number of coupons had to be turned in along with the purchase price. For example, a sirloin steak might cost 13 red stamps, while a can of fruit cocktail might cost 10 blue stamps. These rationing schedules changed often due to supply and demand.

Assignment

Make a poster about rationing. Remind citizens to do their part in supporting the war effort.

Extension

Make a patriotic poster or a military recruitment poster. Sketch your first draft below.

Culminating Activities

History Day

Set aside a day or morning to devote to activities related to your study of 20th century conflicts.

Parent Help

Encourage parents or adult family members to help set up, monitor, and enjoy the activities. See if they have any special talents, interests, or hobbies that would be a match for specific centers.

Uniforms

Many of your students will have access to military uniforms worn by their parents, grandparents, older siblings, and other relatives. Encourage students to celebrate their family's service by wearing these uniforms or bringing them to share on history day.

Eat Hearty

Plan a luncheon with a patriotic theme. Have students make table decorations at one of the centers. Make sure students do not have any food allergies or dietary restrictions.

Centers

The centers you set up should relate in some way to the conflicts of the 20th century, daily life during that time, or activities from this book. Centers should involve small groups of six or seven students doing an activity and/or making something they can display. Each center should take about 20 minutes after which time students should rotate to the next activity. The following are suggestions for various centers. You may add others for which you have special expertise.

☐ **Flight Center**—In this center students make and test-fly a variety of paper airplanes, using the designs in the book.

☐ **Games and Sports**— Play board games such as Monopoly, Life, Chinese checkers, chess, and checkers which were popular during World War II, or have the class play a game of baseball using softballs or Nerf™ balls.

☐ **Map Making**—Use the map section of this book for map examples and find others in atlases, encyclopedias, and the Internet. The maps can be drawn on tag board, large construction paper, or built in three-dimensional form using clay or salt and flour.

☐ **Plant a Victory Garden**—Have students plant a small vegetable garden. Use fast growing seeds such as radishes, lettuce, beans, and peas. Victory gardens were grown during the war years to increase the food supply.

☐ **Readers' Theater**—This center involves practicing for a readers' theater presentation. Students can use a script in this book or one they wrote and then present it to parents or other classes.

☐ **Reconstruct a Battlefield**—Students at this center will reconstruct a battlefield using modeling clay, craft sticks, sand, small pieces of fabric, felt, construction paper, and/or small branches. Students will need books or pictures of various battlefields. A variety of battlefield maps could be created in a center.

Annotated Bibliography

Nonfiction

Allen, Peter. *The Origins of World War II*. Bookwright, 1992. (Scholarly account of the events leading up to World War II)

Butterfield, Moira. *Going to War in World War II*. Franklin Watts, 2001. (Highly illustrated, colorful book featuring the weapons and battles of World War II)

Clarke, John D. (Ed.). *First World War*. Harcourt, 1995. (Thorough account of World War I)

Cooper, Michael. *Remembering Manzanar: Life in a Japanese Relocation Camp*. Clarion, 2002. (A superb account with many photos of life for ordinary people living in the camp)

Feldman, Ruth Tenzer. *World War I: Chronicle of America's Wars*. Lerner, 2004. (Outstanding account of World War I with special attention to America's role in the conflict)

Frank, Anne. *The Diary of a Young Girl*. Doubleday, 1967.

Gourley, Catherine. *Welcome to Molly's World, 1944: Growing Up in World War II America*. American Girls Collection, Pleasant, 1999. (Great pictures and accounts of life on the home front)

Hamilton, John. *Battles of World War I*. ABDO, 2004. (Clear, brief accounts of the major battles of the war)

Hamilton, John. *Events Leading to World War I*. ABDO, 2004. (Exceptionally clear account of the events which led up to World War I)

Knapp, Ron. *American Generals of World War II*. Enslow, 1998. (Good collective biography of the major generals)

Krull, Kathleen. *V is for Victory*. Knopf, 1995. (A well-illustrated, detailed account of many facets of World War II life at home and in the services)

Panchyk, Richard. *World War II for Kids*. Chicago Review Press, 2002. (An outstanding overview of the war for upper middle grade children with activities designed to help children understand rationing, bombing, bandaging, and recruiting)

Rees, Rosemary. *The Western Front*. Rigby, 1997. (Very thoughtful explanations and a thought-provoking look at some source documents)

Ross, Stewart. *Causes and Consequences of World War I*. Raintree, 1998. (A detailed account of the events leading up to World War I)

Weapons of War: World War II. Lucent, 2000. (An excellent description of the weapons used in this war by many countries)

Whitman, Sylvia. *Children of the World War II Home Front*. Carolrhoda, 2001. (A very easy-to-read pictorial account of life on the home front in America)

Fiction

Coerr, Eleanor. *Sadako and the Thousand Paper Cranes*. Putnam, 1977.

Hesse, Karen. *Letters from Rifka*. Holt, 1992.

Houston, Jeanne Wakatsuki and James Houston. *Farewell to Manzanar*. Houghton, 1973.

Lowry, Lois. *Number the Stars*. Houghton, 1989.

Multimedia

Cold War Multimedia Collection CD. Teacher Created Resources. TCR3453.

World War I Multimedia Collection CD. Teacher Created Resources. TCR3042.

World War II Multimedia Collection CD. Teacher Created Resources. TCR3043.

Glossary

alliance—an agreement between countries, often to defend each other in time of war

Allies—the nations who fought against the Central powers in World War I and the Axis powers in World War II

armistice—a cease-fire or peace agreement ending a war

armor—steel plating on tanks and ships

assassinate—to murder, oftentimes a political leader

Axis powers—Germany, Japan, and Italy in World War II

blitzkrieg—"lightning war" waged by Germany

blockade—the blocking of a harbor by warships

casualties—dead and injured soldiers or civilians

Central powers—Germany and its allies in World War I

civilian—someone not in the military

communism—a political system in which the state owns all property and controls people's lives

concentration camps—slave labor camps used to exterminate Jews and other minorities

convoy—a group of ships sailing together for protection

D-Day—allied landing at Normandy on June 6, 1944

destroyer—a surface ship which hunts submarines

dictator—an absolute ruler

draft—a procedure for selecting young men for the army

fascism—a nationalistic dictatorship which controls everything in a country

genocide—the killing of a people based on race or religion

ghetto—an small area of a city where a minority group lives

G.I.—"government issue," a nickname for an American soldier

holocaust—the murder of millions of Jews by the Nazis

home front—civilians who support and help with the war effort

kamikaze—Japanese suicide pilots

mobilize—to prepare an army for war

Nazi—a member of Hitler's National Socialist Party

propaganda—false or distorted information

radar—a detection system using radio waves

refugees—people forced to flee their own country

reparations—money or goods paid by the defeated nation of a war

rationing—limiting food or goods

resistance—people who fought against occupying forces

trench—a ditch dug and used by soldiers for protection

ultimatum—a final demand to try and prevent conflict

Answer Key

Page 28
1. b
2. c
3. d
4. c
5. a
6. b
7. b
8. c
9. a
10. d

Page 29
1. b
2. d
3. c
4. b
5. a
6. c
7. b
8. a
9. d
10. a

Page 30
1. b
2. c
3. d
4. d
5. a
6. b
7. a
8. c
9. d
10. a

Page 31
1. a
2. d
3. a
4. c
5. d
6. b
7. c
8. b
9. b
10. d

Page 32
1. d
2. c
3. c
4. b
5. a
6. b
7. c
8. a
9. d
10. b

Page 33
1. a
2. d
3. a
4. b
5. a
6. b
7. d
8. c
9. c
10. a

Page 34
1. b
2. c
3. b
4. d
5. c
6. a
7. a
8. b
9. d
10. a

Page 35
1. d
2. b
3. c
4. d
5. a
6. b
7. a
8. c
9. a
10. b

Page 39
1. tank
2. submarine
3. land mine
4. destroyer
5. bomber
6. jet fighter
7. machine gun
8. bayonet
9. depth charge
10. torpedo
11. bazooka

Answer Key (cont.)

12. hand grenade
13. aircraft carrier
14. radar
15. sonar

Page 40

1. j
2. p
3. o
4. l
5. g
6. n
7. r
8. b
9. m
10. s
11. k
12. c
13. t
14. h
15. d
16. e
17. q
18. i
19. f
20. a

Page 43

Comprehension Questions

1. She didn't know the value of the money she had.
2. Nathan because he is kind to her.
3. She values their efforts and culture.
4. in a book of poems by Pushkin
5. learning languages
6. They work in a clothing factory.
7. to avoid serving in the Russian army
8. She looked innocent and harmless and had pretty, blond hair.
9. her hair
10. the person Rifka is writing to in her book

Discussion Questions
(Answers may vary.)

1. They were fearful of having to support people with charity.
2. She had to be able to be married or she might end up needing charity.
3. The Jews were a scapegoat for Russians unhappy with their way of life.
4. Pushkin is a poet. He writes of the meaning of life.
5. Answers will vary.
6. She is impulsive as in the orange incident and selfish at times.
7. Answers will vary.
8. They were deadly, and little could be done to avoid them.
9. Rifka was very kind to the baby and to Ilya.
10. Answers will vary.

Page 44

Comprehension Questions

1. Annemarie
2. Ellen
3. They are made of fish skin.
4. sugar, flour, meat, electricity, cigarettes, butter
5. He showed them a picture of Lise.
6. It contained a chemical needed to fool the dogs.
7. food, clothes, and supplies
8. She said the aunt died of typhus.
9. bread
10. Sweden
11. the necklace
12. on Henrik's boat

Discussion Questions
(Answers may vary.)

1. They wanted freedom from the Germans.
2. You cannot go out at night. You can be arrested or killed for no reason.
3. It showed discourtesy and contempt.
4. He comes and goes at odd hours. He brings beer and the resistance newspaper.
5. stopped citizens, arrested people, and relocated Jews
6. The Jews were blamed for Germany's failures. They were accused of controlling banks, businesses, and money.

Answer Key *(cont.)*

7. so they would not suspect her

8. Answers will vary.

Page 45

Page 50

Comprehension Questions

1. 1942

2. second-generation Japanese, the children of immigrants

3. Papa

4. "If your parents were fighting, who would you want to die?"

5. Jeanne helps in the house, walks with friends, goes to school and church, and learns from others.

6. He is against it.

7. They earned many decorations for valor.

8. Papa's ancestral home (and his aunt)

9. baton-twirling

10. a friend in junior high school

Discussion Questions

(Answers may vary.)

1. to avoid being suspected of supporting the Japanese

2. They were not allowed to become citizens.

3. Yes, other immigrants were not relocated or arrested.

4. Answers will vary.

5. They lost homes, boats, furniture, land, and jobs.

6. Papa is often erratic but capable of doing many jobs in business, farming, and fishing.

7. Papa's samurai pride often made him unwilling to compromise or accept discourteous behavior.

8. the primitive living conditions, poor food, toilet facilities, loneliness, and embarrassment

9. to hide his shame and anger

10. Jeanne is Japanese, and Americans still distrust them.

Page 51

Comprehension Questions

1. The story is true.

2. Sadako's grandmother

3. Sadako's best friend

4. running

5. leukemia

6. making 1,000 cranes will cure an illness

7. a boy in the hospital who also has leukemia

8. 644

9. Oct. 25, 1955

10. 356

Discussion Questions

(Answers may vary.)

1. to lift her spirits

2. She is energetic and impatient.

3. The food and kimono were special things and a strain on the family budget.

4. She stumbles often.

5. Making the cranes helped lift Sadako's spirits.

6. Wars have effects long after they are over.

7. It is a memorial for those who died in the two atomic explosions in early August.

8. It was such a terrible explosion.

9. Answers will vary.

10. Many children and adults got cancer. Many people had relatives at the sites of the blasts.

Page 66

Allied powers: Belgium, France, Great Britain, Greece, Italy, Romania, Russia, Serbia (Not shown on the map: Australia, Canada, Japan, New Zealand, the United States)

Central powers: Austria-Hungary, Bulgaria, Germany, Ottoman Empire (Turkey)

Answer Key *(cont.)*

Neutral countries: Albania, Denmark, Finland, Luxemburg, Netherlands, Norway, Spain, Sweden, Switzerland

Page 68

Albania, Bulgaria, Czechoslovakia, East Germany, Hungary, Poland, Romania, Yugoslavia

Page 69

1. Saudi Arabia
2. Jordan, Lebanon, Syria
3. Iran, Iraq, Kuwait, Qatar, Saudi Arabia, United Arab Emirates
4. Israel, Lebanon, Syria, Turkey
5. Oman, Yemen
6. Black Sea
7. Caspian Sea

Page 77

1. d
2. e
3. b
4. j
5. h
6. i
7. g
8. f
9. a
10. c
11. k
12. l

Page 84

1. 28.6% or 29%
2. 21.4% or 21%
3. 9,150,000
4. 7,142,558
5. 22,850,000
6. 90%
7. 3,386,200
8. 73.3% or 73%
9. 357,110
10. 20,000

Page 85

1. 19,000
2. 21,300,000
3. 3,100,000 or 3.1 million
4. 20,893,000
5. 7,060,000
6. 8,676,000
7. 33.1% or 33%
8. 87.6% or 88%
9. 3.8% or 4%
10. 13.46% or 13%

Page 86

1. 15,274,497
2. 12.4% or 12%
3. 4.7% or 5%
4. 2,987,857
5. .164% or .2%
6. 27.49% or 27.5%
7. 370,000
8. 29.7% or 30%
9. 39. 47% or 39.5%
10. 11.7 million

Page 87

Extension

Illinois–Chicago Colleens, Peoria Redwings, Rockford Peaches, Springfield Sallies

Indiana–Fort Wayne Daisies, South Bend Blue Sox

Michigan–Battle Creek Belles, Grand Rapids Chicks, Kalamazoo Lassies, Muskegon Belles, Muskegon Lassies

Minnesota–Minneapolis Millerettes

Wisconsin–Kenosha Comets, Milwaukee Chicks, Racine Belles